i**H**uman

成
为
更
好
的
人

BOB DYLAN
THE LYRICS 1961–2012
鲍勃·迪伦诗歌集

暴雨将至

[美] 鲍勃·迪伦　著

奚密　陈黎　张芬龄　译

广西师范大学出版社
·桂林·

BAOYU JIANG ZHI

LYRICS: 1961-2012
著作权合同登记号桂图登字：20-2017-053 号

图书在版编目（CIP）数据

鲍勃·迪伦诗歌集：1961—2012. 暴雨将至：汉英
对照 /（美）鲍勃·迪伦著；奚密，陈黎，张芬龄译.
桂林：广西师范大学出版社，2017.6（2019.6 重印）
书名原文：LYRICS: 1961-2012
ISBN 978-7-5495-9684-3

Ⅰ.①鲍… Ⅱ.①鲍…②奚…③陈…④张…
Ⅲ.①诗集－美国－现代－汉、英 Ⅳ.①I712.25

中国版本图书馆 CIP 数据核字（2017）第 078984 号

出　　版：广西师范大学出版社
　　　　　广西桂林市五里店路 9 号　邮政编码：541004
网　　址：http://www.bbtpress.com
出版人：张艺兵
发　　行：广西师范大学出版社
　　　　　电话：（0773）2802178
印　　刷：山东临沂新华印刷物流集团有限责任公司印刷
　　　　　山东临沂高新技术产业开发区新华路
　　　　　邮政编码：276017
开　　本：740 mm×1 092 mm　　1/32
印　　张：7.25　　　　　字数：85 千字
版　　次：2017 年 6 月第 1 版　　2019 年 6 月第 5 次
定　　价：25.00 元

如发现印装质量问题，影响阅读，请与出版社发行部门联系调换。

目 录

鲍勃·迪伦

附加早期歌词

自由不羁的鲍勃·迪伦

Big City Blues by Bob Dylan 1961

I been thinkin' about you darlin'
You been on my mind
But i cant stay long in this here town
I ain't the settlin' kind
Rain is crashin on the roof
My boots ~~are so soggy~~ feel hot as coals
Got to keep movin' on
You know i got to go

Goin' to New York city
Gonna find my way
Gonna play in the biggest nightclu
underneath the lights of ol'Broadway
Heard lots a things about that big town
Heard the streets are ~~lined with~~ full of gold
Gonna dig me up a brick take it to the bank
gonna roll, jelly roll

鲍勃·迪伦
Bob Dylan

奚密 译

　　1961 年 9 月，年仅二十岁的鲍勃·迪伦在纽约市认识了音乐制作人约翰·韩门德（John H. Hammond），并由其引荐，与哥伦比亚唱片公司签下一纸五年合约。同年 11 月 20、22 日两天，迪伦录制了十三首歌，收入他的第一张专辑，于 1962 年 3 月 19 日发行。

　　专辑的曲风包括传统民谣、当代民歌以及蓝调，而迪伦的原创作品只有两首：《献给伍迪的歌》和《说唱纽约》。"伍迪"即美国著名民谣歌手伍迪·格思里（Woody Guthrie），他心系底层民众，写下了数百首歌曲，其中不乏经典之作，深刻地影响了 20 世纪五六十年代的美国乐坛，被迪伦视为偶像。至于《说唱纽约》，则明显是根据迪伦的"北漂"经验而作。1960 年冬，他从明尼苏达州来到纽约，有一年多的时间穷得连公寓都租不起，只能辗转在不同朋友家里睡沙发。第一张专辑虽然销路不佳，但得到《纽约时报》的好评，迪伦也因此第一次拥有自己的公寓，地址是纽约市第四街西段 161 号。两年后他发行了第二张专辑，其封面就是在此公寓外的街角拍摄的。

　　需要说明的是，本书中，除《说唱纽约》和《献给伍迪的歌》之外的二十七首歌，都是多年后重新发行时放进去的。这些歌曲均为迪伦 20 世纪 60 年代初的作品，有的针砭时事，有的侧写人物，有的歌唱流浪。在录制原专辑时它们没有被收入其中，根据迪伦的说法，他不愿意在第一张专辑里便把自己全部呈现出来。从另一个角度来看，我们也可以说，当时他还处于摸索和尝试的阶段，可能对自己的作品还没有完全的把握，所以唱的多半是别人的歌。从第二张专辑起，他唱的几乎都是自己的作品，而且好歌连连，在短短几年里奠定了他在歌坛的地位。1962 年 4 月，迪伦坐在住家附近的咖啡馆里写下经典作品《在风中飘荡》。

奚密

说唱纽约

从荒野西部流浪到此
离开了我最爱的家乡
自以为经历了苦与甜
直到我进了纽约城里
老百姓往地的底层走
栋栋高楼却往天上建

纽约城里的冬日时节
寒风吹起雪花处处飞
走在街头我无处可去
有人可能冻到骨子里
冻到骨子里的人是我
《纽约时报》说这是十七年来最冷的冬天
让我觉得没那么冷了

肩上挑着一把旧吉他
我赶上一节地铁车厢
一路摇晃翻滚辗转后
我才踏进纽约市边上
那格林尼治村的土地

我走着走着来到街上
林立咖啡馆中的一家
我上得舞台唱歌弹琴
那边那人说："改天再来吧
你的嗓子像个乡巴佬
我们要的是位民歌手"

好吧，我开始吹口琴维生
吹得肺爆一天才赚一块钱
吹得我内外翻转上下颠倒
那边那人说，他好喜欢
不停地说他爱我的琴声
吹一天一块钱也算值了

好几个星期我就这么过
终于在纽约城找到工作
地方大些，赚钱也多些
甚至加入工会交了会费

一个很伟大的人曾经说过
有些人抢劫只用一支钢笔
要不了多久我就明白了
他这句话的意思何在

很多人餐桌上没有丰盛的食物

他们却拥有很多刀与叉

那些刀叉总会派上用场

所以一个阳光温暖的早晨

我漫步走出了那纽约城

鸭舌帽低低地戴在眉上

我的方向是西部的天空

再见了纽约市

你好东奥兰治[1]

---

1. 东奥兰治，位于美国新泽西州埃塞克斯县。当时伍迪·格思里因亨廷顿舞蹈症住院，每逢周末友人格利森夫妇（Bob & Sidsel Gleason）都会将其接到他们东奥兰治的家里。1964 年 1 月 29 日，迪伦在周日的接待中拜会了格思里。

Talking New York

Ramblin' outa the wild West
Leavin' the towns I love the best
Thought I'd seen some ups and downs
'Til I come into New York town
People goin' down to the ground
Buildings goin' up to the sky

Wintertime in New York town
The wind blowin' snow around
Walk around with nowhere to go
Somebody could freeze right to the bone
I froze right to the bone
New York Times said it was the coldest winter in seventeen
    years
I didn't feel so cold then

I swung onto my old guitar
Grabbed hold of a subway car
And after a rocking, reeling, rolling ride
I landed up on the downtown side
Greenwich Village

I walked down there and ended up
In one of them coffee-houses on the block
Got on the stage to sing and play
Man there said, "Come back some other day
You sound like a hillbilly
We want folk singers here"

Well, I got a harmonica job, begun to play
Blowin' my lungs out for a dollar a day
I blowed inside out and upside down
The man there said he loved m' sound
He was ravin' about how he loved m' sound
Dollar a day's worth

And after weeks and weeks of hangin' around
I finally got a job in New York town
In a bigger place, bigger money too
Even joined the union and paid m' dues

Now, a very great man once said
That some people rob you with a fountain pen
It didn't take too long to find out
Just what he was talkin' about
A lot of people don't have much food on their table
But they got a lot of forks 'n' knives
And they gotta cut somethin'

So one mornin' when the sun was warm
I rambled out of New York town
Pulled my cap down over my eyes
And headed out for the western skies
So long, New York
Howdy, East Orange

献给伍迪的歌

只身在此我远离家乡一千里
走在一条别人都走过的路上
我看见了你世界中的人与事
你的穷人与农人、王子与国王

嗨嗨，伍迪·格思里，我为你写了一首歌
关于前行中的可笑的苍老世界
它似乎病了饿了，累了也破了
看起来它已经要死了却才出生

嗨，伍迪·格思里，但我知道你知道
所有我说的事，而且多过它好几倍
我为你唱首歌，但是我总是唱不够
因为没有多少人做过你做过的事

也献给西斯科、桑尼和铅肚皮 [1]

---

1. 西斯科·休斯顿（Cisco Houston，1918—1961），美国民谣歌手和词作家。桑尼·特里（Sonny Terry，1911—1986），美国山麓蓝调、民谣歌手。铅肚皮（Lead Belly，1885—1949），美国民谣、蓝调歌手，曾因杀人罪被判刑三十年。三人皆与格思里合作过。

也献给所有跟你游历的好人们
献给这些人的心灵与他们的双手
这些随尘土而来又随风归去的人

明天我将离去虽然今天也可以
某一天某条路上走下去
我想做的最后一件事是
说我也曾走过艰苦旅途

Song to Woody

I'm out here a thousand miles from my home
Walkin' a road other men have gone down
I'm seein' your world of people and things
Your paupers and peasants and princes and kings

Hey, hey, Woody Guthrie, I wrote you a song
'Bout a funny ol' world that's a-comin' along
Seems sick an' it's hungry, it's tired an' it's torn
It looks like it's a-dyin' an' it's hardly been born

Hey, Woody Guthrie, but I know that you know
All the things that I'm a-sayin' an' a-many times more
I'm a-singin' you the song, but I can't sing enough
'Cause there's not many men that done the things that
    you've done

Here's to Cisco an' Sonny an' Leadbelly too
An' to all the good people that traveled with you
Here's to the hearts and the hands of the men
That come with the dust and are gone with the wind

I'm a-leavin' tomorrow, but I could leave today
Somewhere down the road someday
The very last thing that I'd want to do
Is to say I've been hittin' some hard travelin' too

纽约城里的苦日子

来吧女士们先生们，听听我的歌
我唱得对，但是你们可能以为错
我只是稍稍讲一个故事
关于你们熟悉的东岸城市
城市里的苦日子
潦倒在纽约城里

老纽约市是一个友善的老城镇
一路从华盛顿高地到哈莱姆区
那么多的人成群结伴四处闲荡
你得意时他们踢你，失意时他们踩你
城市里的苦日子
潦倒在纽约城里

那是多远的距离从金门大桥
到洛克菲勒中心和帝国大厦
洛克菲勒先生高高在上像只鸟
而帝国老先生从来不说一句话
从乡下来的苦日子
潦倒在纽约城里

好吧，早上起床后试着找份工作

在一个地点站久了双脚开始酸痛

若有大把钞票你可令自己很快乐

如果只有五美分，你得乘斯坦顿岛渡轮 [1]

城市里的苦日子

潦倒在纽约城里

赫德森先生顺着河流一路航行

小步舞曲老先生为其梦想付出

买下你的城一条没有回头的路

如果我能做主我会转手再出售

城市里的苦日子

潦倒在纽约城里

我愿意忍受加利福尼亚所有的雾霾

和俄克拉何马平原上的每一粒沙尘

还有落基山矿区山洞里的所有煤渣

它们都比纽约的种种来得干净

城市里的苦日子

潦倒在纽约城里

---

1. 斯坦顿岛渡轮，美国纽约港内往返斯坦顿岛与曼哈顿的客渡轮。早年渡轮
票价五美分，与地铁相比便宜很多。

所以你们所有饶舌的人，四处传播消息
你们可以听听我的故事，听听我的歌
你们可以践踏我的名字，或找人揍我
当我离开纽约后，我会依靠我自己
城市里的苦日子
潦倒在纽约城里

Hard Times in New York Town

Come you ladies and you gentlemen, a-listen to my song
Sing it to you right, but you might think it's wrong
Just a little glimpse of a story I'll tell
'Bout an East Coast city that you all know well
It's hard times in the city
Livin' down in New York town

Old New York City is a friendly old town
From Washington Heights to Harlem on down
There's a-mighty many people all millin' all around
They'll kick you when you're up and knock you when
    you're down
It's hard times in the city
Livin' down in New York town

It's a mighty long ways from the Golden Gate
To Rockefeller Plaza 'n' the Empire State
Mister Rockefeller sets up as high as a bird
Old Mister Empire never says a word
It's hard times from the country
Livin' down in New York town

Well, it's up in the mornin' tryin' to find a job of work
Stand in one place till your feet begin to hurt
If you got a lot o' money you can make yourself merry
If you only got a nickel, it's the Staten Island Ferry
And it's hard times in the city
Livin' down in New York town

Mister Hudson come a-sailin' down the stream
And old Mister Minuet paid for his dream
Bought your city on a one-way track
'F I had my way I'd sell it right back
And it's hard times in the city
Livin' down in New York town

I'll take all the smog in Cal-i-for-ne-ay
'N' every bit of dust in the Oklahoma plains
'N' the dirt in the caves of the Rocky Mountain mines
It's all much cleaner than the New York kind
And it's hard times in the city
Livin' down in New York town

So all you newsy people, spread the news around
You c'n listen to m' story, listen to m' song
You c'n step on my name, you c'n try 'n' get me beat
When I leave New York, I'll be standin' on my feet
And it's hard times in the city
Livin' down in New York town

说唱熊山野餐惨案蓝调 [1]

有一天我看到一则广告
熊山野餐的日子快到了
"来呀来出游
我们用船载你过去
带着你的妻子儿女
带着你的全家人"
太棒了!

所以我立刻跑去买票
一张去熊山野餐的票
但是我从没想到
会碰上一场野餐意外
那跟高山没任何关系
我连一只野熊都没靠近

带着妻子儿女来到码头
有六千个人聚集在那里

---

1. 1961 年 6 月 18 日,在沿哈德逊河坐船到纽约市北部熊山州立公园的一次
郊游中,有人贩卖假票,导致乘客太多,船不胜负荷而沉没,造成多人死伤。

人手一张郊游的票

"好啊，"我说，"那船够大

况且，反正人愈多愈欢乐"

哎呀，谁知道当我们上了船

那艘老旧的大船开始下沉

乘客还是不断地挤上来

那艘老船慢慢地往下沉

野餐郊游这开头真不妙

哎呀，没多久我的妻儿走失了

我一辈子没看过那么多人

那艘老船沉入水里

六千人好像试图自相残杀

狗在狂吠，猫在咪咪叫

女人尖叫，拳头飞，婴儿哭号

警察正在来的路上，我在狂奔

或许我们这次野餐取消为妙

我被人推挤摔倒在地上

耳朵里我只听到一声尖叫

脑海里其他什么都记不得

只记得醒来后我在岸上

头被打破了，胃受重击
双脚划口子，帽子衣服全没了……
不过能够活着就算幸运

我觉得我刚从棺材里爬出来
手里紧抓着我野餐的藤篮子
带着我的妻儿我们动身回家
真希望那个早晨我没起床

现在我不管你到底想做什么
如果你想去野餐也悉听尊便
但是不要告诉我，我不想听
因为我已失去了野餐的心情
只想待在自己的厨房里，办个野餐……
在浴室里

嗳，对我来说这整件事并不好笑
有些人愿意为了钱不择手段
每天都想出一个新花样
只是为了骗某些人的钱
我觉得我们应该把这样的人
放在船上然后送他们去熊山……
去野餐

Talking Bear Mountain Picnic Massacre Blues

I saw it advertised one day
Bear Mountain picnic was comin' my way
"Come along 'n' take a trip
We'll bring you up there on a ship
Bring the wife and kids
Bring the whole family"
Yippee!

Well, I run right down 'n' bought a ticket
To this Bear Mountain Picnic
But little did I realize
I was in for a picnic surprise
Had nothin' to do with mountains
I didn't even come close to a bear

Took the wife 'n' kids down to the pier
Six thousand people there
Everybody had a ticket for the trip
"Oh well," I said, "it's a pretty big ship
Besides, anyway, the more the merrier"

Well, we all got on 'n' what d'ya think
That big old boat started t' sink
More people kept a-pilin' on
That old ship was a-slowly goin' down
Funny way t' start a picnic

Well, I soon lost track of m' kids 'n' wife
So many people there I never saw in m' life

That old ship sinkin' down in the water
Six thousand people tryin' t' kill each other
Dogs a-barkin', cats a-meowin'
Women screamin', fists a-flyin', babies cryin'
Cops a-comin', me a-runnin'
Maybe we just better call off the picnic

I got shoved down 'n' pushed around
All I could hear there was a screamin' sound
Don't remember one thing more
Just remember wakin' up on a little shore
Head busted, stomach cracked
Feet splintered, I was bald, naked...
Quite lucky to be alive though

Feelin' like I climbed outa m' casket
I grabbed back hold of m' picnic basket
Took the wife 'n' kids 'n' started home
Wishin' I'd never got up that morn

Now, I don't care just what you do
If you wanta have a picnic, that's up t' you
But don't tell me about it, I don't wanta hear it
'Cause, see, I just lost all m' picnic spirit
Stay in m' kitchen, have m' own picnic...
In the bathroom

Now, it don't seem to me quite so funny
What some people are gonna do f'r money
There's a bran' new gimmick every day
Just t' take somebody's money away
I think we oughta take some o' these people
And put 'em on a boat, send 'em up to Bear Mountain...
For a picnic

流浪赌徒威利 [1]

过来，你们这些流浪赌徒，我来讲个故事

关于最伟大的赌徒，你们应该都很了解

他名叫威尔·奥康利，他赌了一辈子

有二十七个儿女，却从没一个老婆

赌一把，威利，赌一把

滚骰子，威利，滚骰子

不管你现在在哪儿赌，没人会知道

他曾经在白宫赌，也在火车站里赌

只要有人的地方就有威利和他的牌

他享有大赌徒之称，周遭无人不晓

当威利进了城，妻子让丈夫待在家里

赌一把，威利，赌一把

滚骰子，威利，滚骰子

不管你现在在哪儿赌，没人会知道

---

1. 歌曲灵感及旋律源自爱尔兰克兰西兄弟乐队（The Clancy Brothers）的歌曲《布伦南在沼泽地》（*Brennan on the Moor*），该曲源出爱尔兰同名传统歌谣，讲述 19 世纪爱尔兰拦路强盗威利·布伦南（Willie Brennan）的故事。

顺着密西西比河航行来到新奥尔良
他们仍在说杰克逊河皇后号的赌场
"我是来赢把钱的。"赌徒威利说
游戏结束时，整艘船已为威利所拥有
赌一把，威利，赌一把
滚骰子，威利，滚骰子
不管你现在在哪儿赌，没人会知道

在落基山上有个小镇叫作瘸子溪
有一个礼拜那里夜夜开通宵赌局
九百个矿工——拿出钱来下赌注
威利终于离开时，整个镇都是他的
赌一把，威利，赌一把
滚骰子，威利，滚骰子
不管你现在在哪儿赌，没人会知道

但是我知道威利有颗黄金一般的心
他养活他所有的儿女和儿女的母亲
他不像别的赌徒那样戴戒指穿华衣
他把钱财博施广布，帮助病人与穷人
赌一把，威利，赌一把
滚骰子，威利，滚骰子
不管你现在在哪儿赌，没人会知道

你跟威利玩牌时，你永远都不知道

他到底是虚张声势呢还是真有好牌

他曾赢过一笔财富，那人座上扔掉一手

方块同花顺，而威利连一个对子都没有

赌一把，威利，赌一把

滚骰子，威利，滚骰子

不管你现在在哪儿赌，没人会知道

某个深夜在一场扑克牌游戏中间

一个输光的赌徒说都是威利的错

一枪打穿了可怜威利的脑袋，命运真不好

当他的牌掉在地上：一对 A 和一对八

赌一把，威利，赌一把

滚骰子，威利，滚骰子

不管你现在在哪儿赌，没人会知道

所以所有的流浪赌徒，无论你们在何处

这个故事的教训再清楚也不过

能赢时就赢，在你必须收手之前

因为当你抽到"死人之手"[1]，赌博的日子也就不再

---

1. 美国西部传奇人物詹姆斯·巴特勒·希科克（James Butler Hickok），1876 年在达科他准州戴德伍德的一家酒馆里被人从背后射杀，死时手里握着四张牌：黑桃 A、梅花 A、黑桃 8、梅花 8，因此被称为"死人之手"。

赌一把，威利，赌一把

滚骰子，威利，滚骰子

不管你现在在哪儿赌，没人会知道

Rambling, Gambling Willie

Come around you rovin' gamblers and a story I will tell
About the greatest gambler, you all should know him well
His name was Will O'Conley and he gambled all his life
He had twenty-seven children, yet he never had a wife
And it's ride, Willie, ride
Roll, Willie, roll
Wherever you are a-gamblin' now, nobody really knows

He gambled in the White House and in the railroad yards
Wherever there was people, there was Willie and his cards
He had the reputation as the gamblin'est man around
Wives would keep their husbands home when Willie came
   to town
And it's ride, Willie, ride
Roll, Willie, roll
Wherever you are a-gamblin' now, nobody really knows

Sailin' down the Mississippi to a town called New Orleans
They're still talkin' about their card game on that Jackson
   River Queen
"I've come to win some money," Gamblin' Willie says
When the game finally ended up, the whole damn boat was
   his
And it's ride, Willie, ride
Roll, Willie, roll
Wherever you are a-gamblin' now, nobody really knows

Up in the Rocky Mountains in a town called Cripple Creek
There was an all-night poker game, lasted about a week

Nine hundred miners had laid their money down
When Willie finally left the room, he owned the whole
   damn town
And it's ride, Willie, ride
Roll, Willie, roll
Wherever you are a-gamblin' now, nobody really knows

But Willie had a heart of gold and this I know is true
He supported all his children and all their mothers too
He wore no rings or fancy things, like other gamblers wore
He spread his money far and wide, to help the sick and the
   poor
And it's ride, Willie, ride
Roll, Willie, roll
Wherever you are a-gamblin' now, nobody really knows

When you played your cards with Willie, you never really
   knew
Whether he was bluffin' or whether he was true
He won a fortune from a man who folded in his chair
The man, he left a diamond flush, Willie didn't even have
   a pair
And it's ride, Willie, ride
Roll, Willie, roll
Wherever you are a-gamblin' now, nobody really knows

It was late one evenin' during a poker game
A man lost all his money, he said Willie was to blame
He shot poor Willie through the head, which was a tragic
   fate
When Willie's cards fell on the floor, they were aces backed
   with eights
And it's ride, Willie, ride

Roll, Willie, roll
Wherever you are a-gamblin' now, nobody really knows

So all you rovin' gamblers, wherever you might be
The moral of the story is very plain to see
Make your money while you can, before you have to stop
For when you pull that dead man's hand, your gamblin'
  days are up
And it's ride, Willie, ride
Roll, Willie, roll
Wherever you are a-gamblin' now, nobody really knows

站在公路边

哦，我站在公路边
试图搭个便车，搭个便车
试图搭个便车
哦，我站在公路边
试图搭个便车，搭个便车
试图搭个便车
似乎没人认得我
人人与我擦肩而过

哦，我站在公路边
试图振作，试图振作
试图勇敢振作
哦，我站在公路边
试图振作，试图勇敢振作
一条大路通向光明的灯火
另一条直抵我的坟墓

哦，我看看这两张牌
它们看似手工做的
哦，我看看这两张牌

它们看似手工做的
一张看起来是方块 A
另一张看起来是黑桃 A

哦，我站在公路边
看着我的生命流逝
哦，我站在公路边
看着我的生命流逝
哦，我站在公路边
试图搭个便车

哦，我站在公路边
好奇人都到哪儿去了，
　好奇人都到哪儿去了
好奇人都到哪儿去了
哦，我站在公路边
好奇人都到哪儿去了，
　好奇人都到哪儿去了
好奇人都到哪儿去了
拜托先生，请让我搭一程
我发誓不会杀任何孩子

我想知道我的好女孩

知不知道我在这儿

好像没有别人知道我的行踪

我想知道我的好女孩

知不知道我在这儿

好像没有别人知道我的行踪

如果她知道我在这儿，上帝

我想知道她会不会祈祷

Standing on the Highway

Well, I'm standin' on the highway
Tryin' to bum a ride, tryin' to bum a ride
Tryin' to bum a ride
Well, I'm standin' on the highway
Tryin' to bum a ride, tryin' to bum a ride
Tryin' to bum a ride
Nobody seem to know me
Everybody pass me by

Well, I'm standin' on the highway
Tryin' to hold up, tryin' to hold up
Tryin' to hold up and be brave
Well, I'm standin' on the highway
Tryin' to hold up, tryin' to hold up and be brave
One road's goin' to the bright lights
The other's goin' down to my grave

Well, I'm lookin' down at two cards
They seem to be handmade
Well, I'm lookin' down at two cards
They seem to be handmade
One looks like it's the ace of diamonds
The other looks like it is the ace of spades

Well, I'm standin' on the highway
Watchin' my life roll by
Well, I'm standin' on the highway
Watchin' my life roll by

Well, I'm standin' on the highway
Tryin' to bum a ride

Well, I'm standin' on the highway
Wonderin' where everybody went,
    wonderin' where everybody went
Wonderin' where everybody went
Well, I'm standin' on the highway
Wonderin' where everybody went,
    wonderin' where everybody went
Wonderin' where everybody went
Please mister, pick me up
I swear I ain't gonna kill nobody's kids

I wonder if my good gal
I wonder if she knows I'm here
Nobody else seems to know I'm here
I wonder if my good gal
I wonder if she knows I'm here
Nobody else seems to know I'm here
If she knows I'm here, Lawd
I wonder if she said a prayer

穷小孩蓝调

嗯，告诉妈妈
昨夜你在哪里过夜？
你听不见我哭泣吗？
嗯嗯嗯

嘿，告诉我，宝贝
这里发生了什么事？
你听不见我哭泣吗？
嗯嗯嗯

嘿，老火车停一下
让穷小孩搭一程
你听不见我哭泣吗？
嗯嗯嗯

嘿，调酒师先生
我发誓我年纪不太小
你听不见我哭泣吗？
嗯嗯嗯

警察先生，吹你的口哨
我可怜的脚被训练得会跑
你听不见我哭泣吗？
嗯嗯嗯

长途电话接线生
我听说这通电话免费
你听不见我哭泣吗？
嗯嗯嗯

灰烬和钻石
其中的区别我看不出来
你听不见我哭泣吗？
嗯嗯嗯

法官先生和陪审团
你们看不到我的处境吗？
你们听不见我哭泣吗？
嗯嗯嗯

密西西比河
我觉得你流得太快了
你听不见我哭泣吗？
嗯嗯嗯

Poor Boy Blues

Mm, tell mama
Where'd ya sleep last night?
Cain't ya hear me cryin'?
Hm, hm, hm

Hey, tell me baby
What's the matter here?
Cain't ya hear me cryin'?
Hm, hm, hm

Hey, stop you ol' train
Let a poor boy ride
Cain't ya hear me cryin'?
Hm, hm, hm

Hey, Mister Bartender
I swear I'm not too young
Cain't ya hear me cryin'?
Hm, hm, hm

Blow your whistle, policeman
My poor feet are trained to run
Cain't ya hear me cryin'?
Hm, hm, hm

Long-distance operator
I hear this phone call is on the house
Cain't ya hear me cryin'?

Hm, hm, hm

Ashes and diamonds
The diff'rence I cain't see
Cain't ya hear me cryin'?
Hm, hm, hm

Mister Judge and Jury
Cain't you see the shape I'm in?
Don't ya hear me cryin'?
Hm, hm, hm

Mississippi River
You a-runnin' too fast for me
Cain't ya hear me cryin'?
Hm, hm, hm

给一位友人的歌谣

悲哀的我坐在铁轨上
望着那个老烟囱
火车正一去不复回

多年前我们常玩在一起
望着火车穿过小镇
如今那火车却驶向坟场

我们北上旅行到北国
湖溪和矿场多充沛
我没有比他更好的朋友

但某天他出了一件意外
我想我是听一个陌生人说的
我低下了头悄悄地走开

一辆柴油机卡车缓缓驶着
载着一车很重的货
把他留在犹他路上

他们把他送回他的家乡
他的母亲哭泣姐姐悲叹
听着教堂的钟声响起

Ballad for a Friend

Sad I'm a-sittin' on the railroad track
Watchin' that old smokestack
Train is a-leavin' but it won't be back

Years ago we hung around
Watchin' trains roll through the town
Now that train is a-graveyard bound

Where we go up in that North Country
Lakes and streams and mines so free
I had no better friend than he

Something happened to him that day
I thought I heard a stranger say
I hung my head and stole away

A diesel truck was rollin' slow
Pullin' down a heavy load
It left him on a Utah road

They carried him back to his home town
His mother cried, his sister moaned
Listenin' to them church bells tone

街上的人

我来为你唱一首歌，不算长的歌
关于一位从不伤天害理的老人
他的死因没人说得准
某天他们发现他死在街上

哦，一个美好的早晨人群围拢
那个人衣履破烂
人行道上他就那样躺着
他们停下来看一眼就各自走开

哦，警察来了他四处望望
"起来，老头，不然我要把你带走"
他用警棍戳了他一下
老人就从马路牙子滚了下去

哦，警察又戳一下并大声叫道
"叫救护车来，这个人死了"
救护车到，他们把他抬上车
我再也没见到那个人

我为你唱了我的歌，不算长的歌

关于一位从不伤天害理的老人

他的死因没人说得准

某天他们发现他死在街上

Man on the Street

I'll sing you a song, ain't very long
'Bout an old man who never done wrong
How he died nobody can say
They found him dead in the street one day

Well, the crowd, they gathered one fine morn
At the man whose clothes 'n' shoes were torn
There on the sidewalk he did lay
They stopped 'n' stared 'n' walked their way

Well, the p'liceman come and he looked around
"Get up, old man, or I'm a-takin' you down"
He jabbed him once with his billy club
And the old man then rolled off the curb

Well, he jabbed him again and loudly said
"Call the wagon; this man is dead"
The wagon come, they loaded him in
I never saw the man again

I've sung you my song, it ain't very long
'Bout an old man who never done wrong
How he died no one can say
They found him dead in the street one day

埃米特·蒂尔之死 [1]

这件事发生在不久以前的密西西比州
当来自芝加哥的少年走进南方一户人家
这个男孩凄惨的悲剧我至今记忆犹新
他皮肤是黑的他名字是埃米特·蒂尔

有人把他拖到谷仓里将他毒打了一顿
他们说有正当的理由，但我不记得是什么
他们对他施暴的细节太邪恶了我不忍重复
谷仓里在惨叫，外面街上却有笑声

然后在血红的雨中他们把他滚下河湾路
然后把他扔进大河淹没了他痛苦的尖叫
他们之所以在那儿杀他，我可以确定不虚
只是为了杀他而且看着他慢慢死去的乐趣

后来为了平息美国高呼审判的抗议声

1.1955 年 8 月 28 日，在美国密西西比州金钱镇，两个白人谋杀了年仅十四
岁的黑人少年埃米特·蒂尔，却被清一色白人组成的陪审团宣判无罪。此案激
发了 20 世纪 60 年代美国的民权运动。

两兄弟承认杀死了可怜的埃米特·蒂尔
但是陪审团员是两兄弟可怕罪行的帮凶
所以审判是个玩笑，但是好像没人在意

我在晨报上读到新闻，但是我不忍看见
那两兄弟微笑着一起走下法院的楼梯
因为陪审团判他们无罪两兄弟获得自由
蒂尔的尸体还浮在歧视黑人的南方水上

如果你不能抗议如此不公的这类行径
你双眼被死人的泥污蒙蔽了，你的心满是灰
你的手脚必被桎梏，你的血必拒绝流动
因为你让人类堕落到上帝不容的地步！

这首歌只是给所有同胞的一个警醒
这类行径今天仍存在于幽灵般的三 K 党
但是如果我们大伙同心，竭尽一切所能
我们可以让我们伟大的家国更伟大

The Death of Emmett Till

'Twas down in Mississippi not so long ago
When a young boy from Chicago town stepped through a
Southern door
This boy's dreadful tragedy I can still remember well
The color of his skin was black and his name was Emmett
Till

Some men they dragged him to a barn and there they beat
him up
They said they had a reason, but I can't remember what
They tortured him and did some things too evil to repeat
There were screaming sounds inside the barn, there was
laughing sounds out on the street

Then they rolled his body down a gulf amidst a bloody red
rain
And they threw him in the waters wide to cease his
screaming pain
The reason that they killed him there, and I'm sure it ain't
no lie
Was just for the fun of killin' him and to watch him slowly
die

And then to stop the United States of yelling for a trial
Two brothers they confessed that they had killed poor
Emmett Till
But on the jury there were men who helped the brothers
commit this awful crime
And so this trial was a mockery, but nobody seemed to mind

I saw the morning papers but I could not bear to see
The smiling brothers walkin' down the courthouse stairs
For the jury found them innocent and the brothers they
went free
While Emmett's body floats the foam of a Jim Crow
southern sea

If you can't speak out against this kind of thing, a crime
that's so unjust
Your eyes are filled with dead men's dirt, your mind is filled
with dust
Your arms and legs they must be in shackles and chains, and
your blood it must refuse to flow
For you let this human race fall down so God-awful low!

This song is just a reminder to remind your fellow man
That this kind of thing still lives today in that ghost-robed
Ku Klux Klan
But if all of us folks that thinks alike, if we gave all we could
give
We could make this great land of ours a greater place to live

让我死在我的脚步里 [1]

我不会走到地下

只因为有人告诉我死亡近了

我不会让自己低头去死

当我走向坟墓时我会仰着头

让我死在我的脚步里

在我走到地下前

战争的风声和发生过的战争 [2]

生命的意义消失在风中

有些人认为末日就要来临

他们不学习生反而学习死

让我死在我的脚步里

在我走到地下前

我不知道自己聪明与否

但别人骗我时我想我能看得出来

---

1. 歌曲灵感源自美苏冷战期间在美国大量修建的防核尘地下室。

2.《新约·马太福音》24:6，耶稣说："你们也要听见打仗和打仗的风声，总不要惊慌，因为这些事是必须有的，只是末期还没有到。"注释凡涉《圣经》处，译文一律引自和合本，供大致的参照。

如果这场战争来临死亡无所不在
让我死在土地上而不是地下
让我死在我的脚步里
在我走到地下前

总有一些人势必制造恐惧
好多年了他们老在说这场战争
我读过他们所有的论述而我未置一词
但如今上帝啊，听听我可怜的声音
让我死在我的脚步里
在我走到地下前

如果我拥有红宝石、财富和皇冠
我就买下全世界然后重新洗牌
我要把所有的枪支坦克扔进海里
因为它们是过去时代的错误
让我死在我的脚步里
在我走到地下前

让我喝山泉不断涌出的水
让野花香自由流淌在我的血液中
让我睡在你青葱的草原上
让我和我的兄弟和平地走在公路上

让我死在我的脚步里

在我走到地下前

走到你国家土地和太阳的交会点

看看火山口和瀑布奔腾的峡谷

内华达、新墨西哥、亚利桑那、爱达荷

让联邦的每个州深深沁入你们的灵魂

你将死在你的脚步里

在你走到地下前

Let Me Die in My Footsteps

I will not go down under the ground
'Cause somebody tells me that death's comin' 'round
An' I will not carry myself down to die
When I go to my grave my head will be high
Let me die in my footsteps
Before I go down under the ground

There's been rumors of war and wars that have been
The meaning of life has been lost in the wind
And some people thinkin' that the end is close by
'Stead of learnin' to live they are learnin' to die
Let me die in my footsteps
Before I go down under the ground

I don't know if I'm smart but I think I can see
When someone is pullin' the wool over me
And if this war comes and death's all around
Let me die on this land 'fore I die underground
Let me die in my footsteps
Before I go down under the ground

There's always been people that have to cause fear
They've been talking of the war now for many long years
I have read all their statements and I've not said a word
But now Lawd God, let my poor voice be heard
Let me die in my footsteps
Before I go down under the ground

If I had rubies and riches and crowns

I'd buy the whole world and change things around
I'd throw all the guns and the tanks in the sea
For they are mistakes of a past history
Let me die in my footsteps
Before I go down under the ground

Let me drink from the waters where the mountain streams
    flood
Let the smell of wildflowers flow free through my blood
Let me sleep in your meadows with the green grassy leaves
Let me walk down the highway with my brother in peace
Let me die in my footsteps
Before I go down under the ground

Go out in your country where the land meets the sun
See the craters and the canyons where the waterfalls run
Nevada, New Mexico, Arizona, Idaho
Let every state in this union seep down deep in your souls
And you'll die in your footsteps
Before you go down under the ground

宝贝，我想你

有时候我情绪来了，我想离开我寂寞的家
有时候我情绪来了，我想听见奶牛哞哞叫
有时候我情绪来了，我想动身上公路
不过还有，不过还有，我说哦，我说哦，我说
哦宝贝，我想你

有时候我情绪来了，上帝，我的心要溢出
有时候我情绪来了，我想写下我的遗嘱
有时候我情绪来了，我想去山上走走
不过还有，不过还有，我说哦，我说哦，我说
哦宝贝，我想你

有时候我情绪来了，我想躺下来就此死去
有时候我情绪来了，我想登上天
有时候我情绪来了，我想大笑直到流泪
不过还有，我再说一遍，我再说一遍，我说
哦宝贝，我想你

有时候我情绪来了，我想睡在我小马的畜栏里
有时候我情绪来了，我什么事也不想做

有时候我情绪来了，我想像加农炮弹一样地飞
不过还有，不过还有，我说哦，我说哦，我说
哦宝贝，我想你

有时候我情绪来了，我想后退靠在墙上
有时候我情绪来了，我想跑到累得地上爬
有时候我情绪来了，我什么事也不想做
不过还有，不过还有，我说哦，我说哦，我说
哦宝贝，我想你

有时候我情绪来了，我想把房子变个样子
有时候我情绪来了，我想改变一下这个小镇
有时候我情绪来了，我想把这世界变个样子
不过还有，不过还有，我说哦，我说哦，我说
哦宝贝，我想你

Baby, I'm in the Mood for You

Sometimes I'm in the mood, I wanna leave my lonesome
   home
And sometimes I'm in the mood, I wanna hear my milk
   cow moan
And sometimes I'm in the mood, I wanna hit that highway
   road
But then again, but then again, I said oh, I said oh, I said
Oh babe, I'm in the mood for you

Sometimes I'm in the mood, Lord, I had my overflowin' fill
Sometimes I'm in the mood, I'm gonna make out my final
   will
Sometimes I'm in the mood, I'm gonna head for the walkin'
   hill
But then again, but then again, I said oh, I said oh, I said
Oh babe, I'm in the mood for you

Sometimes I'm in the mood, I wanna lay right down and
   die
Sometimes I'm in the mood, I wanna climb up to the sky
Sometimes I'm in the mood, I'm gonna laugh until I cry
But then again, I said again, I said again, I said
Oh babe, I'm in the mood for you

Sometimes I'm in the mood, I'm gonna sleep in my pony's
   stall
Sometimes I'm in the mood, I ain't gonna do nothin' at all
Sometimes I'm in the mood, I wanna fly like a cannonball
But then again, but then again, I said oh, I said oh, I said

Oh babe, I'm in the mood for you

Sometimes I'm in the mood, I wanna back up against the wall
Sometimes I'm in the mood, I wanna run till I have to crawl
Sometimes I'm in the mood, I ain't gonna do nothin' at all
But then again, but then again, I said oh, I said oh, I said
Oh babe, I'm in the mood for you

Sometimes I'm in the mood, I wanna change my house around
Sometimes I'm in the mood, I'm gonna make a change in this here town
Sometimes I'm in the mood, I'm gonna change the world around
But then again, but then again, I said oh, I said oh, I said
Oh babe, I'm in the mood for you

很久以前，很远的地方

为了宣扬和平与博爱
哦，得付出什么代价！
很久以前有人这么做
结果被钉上十字架
很久以前，很远的地方
这些事不再发生
如今不再发生

奴隶们的铁链
在地上拖着走
他们垂着头心情低落
但那是林肯的时代
那是很久以前
很久以前，很远的地方
那样的事不再发生
如今不再发生

战争的枪炮狂轰滥炸
整个世界都在流血
尸体漂浮在泥泞

堆积的海洋岸边
很久以前，很远的地方
那些事不再发生
如今不再发生

这个人家财万贯
那个人吃不饱饭
这个人过得如同国王
那个人在街上乞讨
很久以前，很远的地方
那样的事不再发生
如今不再发生

这个人死于一把尖刀
那个人死于一颗子弹
这个人死于破碎的心
眼见爱子被私刑处决
很久以前，很远的地方
那样的事不再发生
如今不再发生

角斗士自相厮杀
那是古罗马时代的事

人们眼红嘴咧地欢呼
当眼睛和心都瞎了
很久以前，很远的地方
那样的事不再发生
如今不再发生

为了论说和平与博爱
哦，得付出什么代价！
很久以前有人这么做
结果被钉上十字架
很久以前，很远的地方
那样的事不再发生
如今不再，是吗？

Long Ago, Far Away

To preach of peace and brotherhood
Oh, what might be the cost!
A man he did it long ago
And they hung him on a cross
Long ago, far away
These things don't happen
No more, nowadays

The chains of slaves
They dragged the ground
With heads and hearts hung low
But it was during Lincoln's time
And it was long ago
Long ago, far away
Things like that don't happen
No more, nowadays

The war guns they went off wild
The whole world bled its blood
Men's bodies floated on the edge
Of oceans made of mud
Long ago, far away
Those kind of things don't happen
No more, nowadays

One man had much money
One man had not enough to eat
One man he lived just like a king
The other man begged on the street

Long ago, far away
Things like that don't happen
No more, nowadays

One man died of a knife so sharp
One man died from the bullet of a gun
One man died of a broken heart
To see the lynchin' of his son
Long ago, far away
Things like that don't happen
No more, nowadays

Gladiators killed themselves
It was during the Roman times
People cheered with bloodshot grins
As eyes and minds went blind
Long ago, far away
Things like that don't happen
No more, nowadays

And to talk of peace and brotherhood
Oh, what might be the cost!
A man he did it long ago
And they hung him on a cross
Long ago, far away
Things like that don't happen
No more, nowadays, do they?

不会哀悼

是的，我不会再哀悼，不再
不会再哀悼，不再
不会再哀悼，不再
不会再哀悼

弟兄们来吧，来加入乐队
姐妹们来吧，双手拍起来
告诉大地上所有的人
你不会再哀悼

是的，我不会再哀悼，不再
不会再哀悼，不再
不会再哀悼，不再
不会再哀悼

褐色与蓝色黑色与白色
都是单行道上的同一种颜色
我们走得这么远不会回头
而且我不会再哀悼

是的，我不会再哀悼，不再

不会再哀悼，不再

不会再哀悼，不再

我不会再哀悼

我们会通知你的家人

你会吵到掀翻屋顶乃至房子垮下

如果你被打倒又再站起来

我们不会再哀悼

是的，我不会再哀悼，不再

不会再哀悼，不再

不会再哀悼，不再

我不会再哀悼

我们将彻夜唱着这首歌

从午夜开始唱给我的宝贝听

当我死后她会对着你唱

不会再哀悼

是的，我不会再哀悼，不再

不会再哀悼，不再

不会再哀悼，不再

我不会再哀悼

Ain't Gonna Grieve

Well, I ain't a-gonna grieve no more, no more
Ain't a-gonna grieve no more, no more
Ain't a-gonna grieve no more, no more
And ain't a-gonna grieve no more

Come on brothers, join the band
Come on sisters, clap your hands
Tell everybody that's in the land
You ain't a-gonna grieve no more

Well, I ain't a-gonna grieve no more, no more
Ain't a-gonna grieve no more, no more
Ain't a-gonna grieve no more, no more
And ain't a-gonna grieve no more

Brown and blue and white and black
All one color on the one-way track
We got this far and ain't a-goin' back
And I ain't a-gonna grieve no more

Well, I ain't a-gonna grieve no more, no more
Ain't a-gonna grieve no more, no more
Ain't a-gonna grieve no more, no more
I ain't a-gonna grieve no more

We're gonna notify your next of kin
You're gonna raise the roof until the house falls in
If you get knocked down get up again
We ain't a-gonna grieve no more

Well, I ain't a-gonna grieve no more, no more
Ain't a-gonna grieve no more, no more
Ain't a-gonna grieve no more, no more
I ain't a-gonna grieve no more

We'll sing this song all night long
Sing it to my baby from midnight on
She'll sing it to you when I'm dead and gone
Ain't a-gonna grieve no more

Well, I ain't a-gonna grieve no more, no more
Ain't a-gonna grieve no more, no more
Ain't a-gonna grieve no more, no more
I ain't a-gonna grieve no more

吉普赛阿露

如果你要找女朋友，最好找两个
以防万一你碰到吉普赛阿露
她是个流浪女郎她的心也爱流浪
总有人被她抛弃
嘿，在那转角处
吉普赛阿露又不见了
吉普赛阿露又不见了

哦，我看遍了整个国家
只为了寻找吉普赛阿露
去北方找，去南方找
跟随着吉普赛阿露
嘿，在那转角处
吉普赛阿露又不见了
吉普赛阿露又不见了

哦，我得停下来歇一歇
我可怜的脚不如以前
我可怜的脚逐渐疲弱
吉普赛阿露又不见了

嘿，又不见了
吉普赛阿露在转角处
吉普赛阿露在转角处

哦，在老夏延市看见她
我才转头她就开溜
从丹佛镇到威奇托
最近我听说她在阿肯色
嘿，在那转角处
吉普赛阿露又不见了
吉普赛阿露又不见了

哦，让我告诉你如果你这么做
告诉你，你的鞋子会磨破
如果你要把鞋子磨破
试试跟随吉普赛阿露
嘿，又不见了
吉普赛阿露在转角处
吉普赛阿露在转角处

哦，吉普赛阿露，有人告诉我
住在阿灵顿的加勒斯路
阿灵顿的加勒斯路

她又搬到华盛顿

嘿，在那转角处

吉普赛阿露又不见了

吉普赛阿露又不见了

哦，我一路跑到华盛顿

她却去了俄勒冈

放弃步行，我跳上火车

她又搬回加勒斯路

嘿，我赢不了

吉普赛阿露又不见了

吉普赛阿露又不见了

哦，最后听到吉普赛阿露的消息

她在孟菲斯蹲牢房

她抛弃了那么多男孩

一个自杀了

嘿，你赢不了

吉普赛阿露又不见了

吉普赛阿露又不见了

Gypsy Lou

If you getcha one girl, better get two
Case you run into Gypsy Lou
She's a ramblin' woman with a ramblin' mind
Always leavin' somebody behind
Hey, 'round the bend
Gypsy Lou's gone again
Gypsy Lou's gone again

Well, I seen the whole country through
Just to find Gypsy Lou
Seen it up, seen it down
Followin' Gypsy Lou around
Hey, 'round the bend
Gypsy Lou's gone again
Gypsy Lou's gone again

Well, I gotta stop and take some rest
My poor feet are second best
My poor feet are wearin' thin
Gypsy Lou's gone again
Hey, gone again
Gypsy Lou's 'round the bend
Gypsy Lou's 'round the bend

Well, seen her up in old Cheyenne
Turned my head and away she ran
From Denver Town to Wichita
Last I heard she's in Arkansas
Hey, 'round the bend

Gypsy Lou's gone again
Gypsy Lou's gone again

Well, I tell you what if you want to do
Tell you what, you'll wear out your shoes
If you want to wear out your shoes
Try and follow Gypsy Lou
Hey, gone again
Gypsy Lou's 'round the bend
Gypsy Lou's 'round the bend

Well, Gypsy Lou, I been told
Livin' down on Gallus Road
Gallus Road, Arlington
Moved away to Washington
Hey, 'round the bend
Gypsy Lou's gone again
Gypsy Lou's gone again

Well, I went down to Washington
Then she went to Oregon
I skipped the ground and hopped a train
She's back in Gallus Road again
Hey, I can't win
Gypsy Lou's gone again
Gypsy Lou's gone again

Well, the last I heard of Gypsy Lou
She's in a Memphis calaboose
She left one too many a boy behind
He committed suicide
Hey, you can't win
Gypsy Lou's gone again
Gypsy Lou's gone again

离去很久

我的父母温柔地把我养大
我是他们的独生子
我却一心想要去流浪
当我还是个少年
第一次离开家时
我才十三岁出头
妈妈，我的到来很久
我的离去也会很久

在得克萨斯西部
在得克萨斯的平原上
我试着找份工作
但是他们说我年纪小
我眼睛发热当我听到
"哪儿来的回哪儿去！"
我的到来很久
我的离去也会很久

我记得我一路流浪
搭乘嘉年华会的火车

不同的市镇不同的人
然而他们又差不多
记忆最深的是孩子们的脸
我记得一直在旅行
我的到来很久
我的离去也会很久

曾经我爱上一个美丽的姑娘
我也不是太大，可以说出来
如果她伤过我的心一次
她便伤了它十次十二次
我孤独地走路我自言自语
我没告诉任何人
宝贝，我的到来很久
我的离去也会很久

很多次我站在公路旁
试图搭个便车
我的眼睛充血我紧咬着牙
看着车辆驰过
我的脑袋里空空如也
整天我想的是
我的到来很久

我的离去也会很久

你可能在十字路口见过我
当我经过的时候
用你的方式去记得我
当我飘出你的视线
我没有时间去想这些
我有太多要做的事
是的，我的到来很久
我的离去也会很久

如果我不能帮助别人
用一个字或一首歌
如果我不能向别人指明
他们走的是一条歧途
但我知道我不是先知
也不是先知的儿子
只是我的到来很久
我的离去也会很久

所以你可以有你的美丽
它很肤浅它只会撒谎
你也可以拥有青春

它将在你眼前腐败

不妨给我一块墓碑

上面清楚刻着：

"我的到来很久

我的离去也会很久"

Long Time Gone

My parents raised me tenderly
I was their only son
My mind got mixed with ramblin'
When I was all so young
And I left my home the first time
When I was twelve and one
I'm a long time a-comin', Maw
An' I'll be a long time gone

On the western side of Texas
On the Texas plains
I tried to find a job o' work
But they said I's young of age
My eyes they burned when I heard
"Go home where you belong!"
I'm a long time a-comin'
An' I'll be a long time gone

I remember when I's ramblin'
Around with the carnival trains
Different towns, different people
Somehow they're all the same
I remember children's faces best
I remember travelin' on
I'm a long time a-comin'
I'll be a long time gone

I once loved a fair young maid
An' I ain't too big to tell

If she broke my heart a single time
She broke it ten or twelve
I walked and talked all by myself
I did not tell no one
I'm a long time a-comin', babe
An' I'll be a long time gone

Many times by the highwayside
I tried to flag a ride
With bloodshot eyes and gritting teeth
I'd watch the cars roll by
The empty air hung in my head
I's thinkin' all day long
I'm a long time a-comin'
I'll be a long time gone

You might see me on your crossroads
When I'm a-passin' through
Remember me how you wished to
As I'm a-driftin' from your view
I ain't got the time to think about it
I got too much to get done
Well, I'm a long time comin'
An' I'll be a long time gone

If I can't help somebody
With a word or song
If I can't show somebody
They are travelin' wrong
But I know I ain't no prophet
An' I ain't no prophet's son
I'm just a long time a-comin'
An' I'll be a long time gone

So you can have your beauty
It's skin deep and it only lies
And you can have your youth
It'll rot before your eyes
Just give to me my gravestone
With it clearly carved upon:
"I's a long time a-comin'
An' I'll be a long time gone"

沿路走下去

是的，我沿路走下去
我沿路走下去
而且我沿路走下去
双脚会飞奔起来
诉说我烦忧的心

我有一个昏沉沉的女友
我有一个昏沉沉的女友
我有一个昏沉沉的女友
她觉得不舒服
何时会好只有时间知道

是的，我沿路走下去
我沿路走下去
而且我沿路走下去
双脚会飞奔起来
诉说我烦忧的心

我的钱来了又走
我的钱来了又走

我的钱来了又走

它滚来又流走，滚来又流走

从我衣服口袋的破洞

是的，我沿路走下去

我沿路走下去

而且我沿路走下去

双脚会飞奔起来

诉说我烦忧的心

我看见一道晨光

我看见一道晨光

并不是因为

我是个早起的人

昨晚我整夜没合眼

是的，我沿路走下去

我沿路走下去

而且我沿路走下去

双脚会飞奔起来

诉说我烦忧的心

我有我的步行鞋

我有我的步行鞋

我有我的步行鞋

我就不会输

我想我有步行蓝调

是的，我沿路走下去

我沿路走下去

而且我沿路走下去

双脚会飞奔起来

诉说我烦忧的心

Walkin' Down the Line

Well, I'm walkin' down the line
I'm walkin' down the line
An' I'm walkin' down the line
My feet'll be a-flyin'
To tell about my troubled mind

I got a heavy-headed gal
I got a heavy-headed gal
I got a heavy-headed gal
She ain't a-feelin' well
When she's better only time will tell

Well, I'm walkin' down the line
I'm walkin' down the line
An' I'm walkin' down the line
My feet'll be a-flyin'
To tell about my troubled mind

My money comes and goes
My money comes and goes
My money comes and goes
And rolls and flows and rolls and flows
Through the holes in the pockets in my clothes

Well, I'm walkin' down the line
I'm walkin' down the line
An' I'm walkin' down the line
My feet'll be a-flyin'
To tell about my troubled mind

I see the morning light
I see the morning light
Well, it's not because
I'm an early riser
I didn't go to sleep last night

Well, I'm walkin' down the line
I'm walkin' down the line
An' I'm walkin' down the line
My feet'll be a-flyin'
To tell about my troubled mind

I got my walkin' shoes
I got my walkin' shoes
I got my walkin' shoes
An' I ain't a-gonna lose
I believe I got the walkin' blues

Well, I'm walkin' down the line
I'm walkin' down the line
An' I'm walkin' down the line
My feet'll be a-flyin'
To tell about my troubled mind

旅行火车

有一列铁皮旅行火车驶过许多年头
它的锅炉充满着恨，它的火炉充满恐惧
如果你曾听见其声音或看见血红的破支架
那么你就听过我的歌声知道我的名字

你曾停下来好奇它包藏了什么仇恨吗？
你曾看见它的乘客疯狂混乱的灵魂吗？
你曾动念想过你必须让那火车停下来吗？
那么你就听过我的歌声知道我的名字

你可曾厌倦了恐惧那说教的声声
当它锤你的脑袋敲打你的耳朵？
你可曾问过它是什么却得不到明确的回答？
那么你就听过我的歌声知道我的名字

我很好奇世界各国的领袖是否明白
他们留给我手上这满是杀戮的世界？
午夜无眠时你可曾有过同样的疑问？
那么你就曾听过我的歌声知道我的名字

你可曾嘴上这么说或心里这么想

站在你旁边的那个人可能被误导？

那些疯子的叫嚣是否让你内心要发疯？

那么你就曾听过我的歌声知道我的名字

嗜血的强盗和仇恨者让你消沉吗？

那些说教和政治让你晕头转向吗？

公交车被焚毁会让你心痛吗？

那么你就曾听过我的歌声知道我的名字

Train A-Travelin'

There's an iron train a-travelin' that's been a-rollin' through
  the years
With a firebox of hatred and a furnace full of fears
If you ever heard its sound or seen its blood-red broken
  frame
Then you heard my voice a-singin' and you know my name

Did you ever stop to wonder 'bout the hatred that it holds?
Did you ever see its passengers, its crazy mixed-up souls?
Did you ever start a-thinkin' that you gotta stop that train?
Then you heard my voice a-singin' and you know my name

Do you ever get tired of the preachin' sounds of fear
When they're hammered at your head and pounded in your
  ear?
Have you ever asked about it and not been answered plain?
Then you heard my voice a-singin' and you know my name

I'm a-wonderin' if the leaders of the nations understand
This murder-minded world that they're leavin' in my hands
Have you ever laid awake at night and wondered 'bout the
  same?
Then you've heard my voice a-singin' and you know my name

Have you ever had it on your lips or said it in your head
That the person standin' next to you just might be misled?
Does the raving of the maniacs make your insides go insane?
Then you've heard my voice a-singin' and you know my
  name

Do the kill-crazy bandits and the haters get you down?
Does the preachin' and the politics spin your head around?
Does the burning of the buses give your heart a pain?
Then you've heard my voice a-singin' and you know my
name

唐纳德·怀特之歌

我名叫唐纳德·怀特，你看
我站在你们的面前
被你们判为谋杀者
行刑人的绳索必须垂下
我将死在绞刑架上
在明月高照的时候
而这些是我最后的
你们听得见的遗言

离开堪萨斯的家乡
在我很年轻的时候
我踏上老西北土地
华盛顿州的西雅图
虽然走了许多里的路
我从没交到一个朋友
因为生活里遇见的人
我总无法与他们相处

如果我受过些教育
给我一个好的开始

也许我会当名医生
或者成为艺术大师
但是我用双手偷窃
当我很年轻的时候
他们把我关在牢里
我一生就这样开始

哦，监狱里的囚犯
我发现是我的同类
只有在铁栏杆里面
我才找到心灵平静
但是监狱太过拥挤
所有地方人满为患
所以他们把我放回
仓促复杂的人生路

危险存在于海洋上
咸水海浪高高裂开
危险存在于战场上
子弹弹壳四处乱飞
危险在开放的世上
人们努力争取自由
而对我而言最危险的

是置身在这社会中

所以我求他们送我
回那个监狱里的家
但是他们说那里太挤
腾不出地方给我住
我双膝跪下恳求他们
"哦，拜托把我关起来"
但是他们不为所动
也不肯听我的言语

所以就在那圣诞夜
西元一九五九年
晚上我杀了一个人
也没打算隐瞒真相
陪审团判我有罪
我毫无异议
因为我知道我会犯罪
如果不把我关起来

我庆幸我没有父母
照顾我或为我哭泣
现在他们永远不会知道

我将死得多恐怖

我也庆幸我没有朋友

看见我的羞辱

因为他们永远不会看到行刑人

罩在我头上的黑布

再见了老北方的树林

我曾经流连的地方

再见了热闹的酒吧

它们曾经是我的家

再见了所有的人们

你们只想到我的最坏

我想你们会觉得好多了

当我吊在那棵树上

但是我还有一个问题

在他们处死我之前

我好奇的是到底你们

听见多少我说的话

关于所有那些男孩

走上我走过的路

他们是你们这社会的敌人

还是受害人？

Ballad of Donald White

My name is Donald White, you see
I stand before you all
I was judged by you a murderer
And the hangman's knot must fall
I will die upon the gallows pole
When the moon is shining clear
And these are my final words
That you will ever hear

I left my home in Kansas
When I was very young
I landed in the old Northwest
Seattle, Washington
Although I'd a-traveled many miles
I never made a friend
For I could never get along in life
With people that I met

If I had some education
To give me a decent start
I might have been a doctor or
A master in the arts
But I used my hands for stealing
When I was very young
And they locked me down in jailhouse cells
That's how my life begun

Oh, the inmates and the prisoners
I found they were my kind

And it was there inside the bars
I found my peace of mind
But the jails they were too crowded
Institutions overflowed
So they turned me loose to walk upon
Life's hurried tangled road

And there's danger on the ocean
Where the salt sea waves split high
And there's danger on the battlefield
Where the shells of bullets fly
And there's danger in this open world
Where men strive to be free
And for me the greatest danger
Was in society

So I asked them to send me back
To the institution home
But they said they were too crowded
For me they had no room
I got down on my knees and begged
"Oh, please put me away"
But they would not listen to my plea
Or nothing I would say

And so it was on Christmas Eve
In the year of '59
It was on that night I killed a man
I did not try to hide
The jury found me guilty
And I won't disagree
For I knew that it would happen
If I wasn't put away

And I'm glad I've had no parents
To care for me or cry
For now they will never know
The horrible death I die
And I'm also glad I've had no friends
To see me in disgrace
For they'll never see that hangman's hood
Wrap around my face

Farewell unto the old north woods
Of which I used to roam
Farewell unto the crowded bars
Of which've been my home
Farewell to all you people
Who think the worst of me
I guess you'll feel much better when
I'm on that hanging tree

But there's just one question
Before they kill me dead
I'm wondering just how much
To you I really said
Concerning all the boys that come
Down a road like me
Are they enemies or victims
Of your society?

戒掉你的恶劣行径

哦，你可以大声朗读你的《圣经》
你可以双膝跪下，漂亮妈妈[1]
然后向上帝祷告
但是这些都没有帮助。

你会需要
总有一天你会需要我帮忙
是的，如果你没法戒掉你的罪恶
请你戒掉你的恶劣行径

是的，你可以跑到白宫那里
可以眺望国会大厦的圆顶，漂亮妈妈
你可以猛敲总统先生的大门
但是现在你该知道一切都太晚了

你会需要
总有一天你会需要我帮忙
是的，如果你没法戒掉你的罪恶

---

1. 妈妈，口语中又有"情人""妻子"之意。

请你戒掉你的恶劣行径

是的，你可以跑到沙漠里
倒下躺在炽热的沙上
你可以举起你的右手，漂亮妈妈
但是你最好明白你失去了一个好男人

你会需要
总有一天你会需要我帮忙
是的，如果你没法戒掉你的罪恶
请你戒掉你的恶劣行径

还有你可以去公路搭便车
你可以孤独地站在路边
你可以挥辆车回家，漂亮妈妈
但是你再也不能搭我的车了

你会需要
总有一天你会需要我帮忙
是的，如果你没法戒掉你的罪恶
请你戒掉你的恶劣行径

哦，你可以大声朗读你的《圣经》

你可以双膝跪下，漂亮妈妈

然后向上帝祷告

但是这些都没有帮助

你会需要

总有一天你会需要我帮忙

是的，如果你没法戒掉你的罪恶

请你戒掉你的恶劣行径

Quit Your Low Down Ways

Oh, you can read out your Bible
You can fall down on your knees, pretty mama
And pray to the Lord
But it ain't gonna do no good.

You're gonna need
You're gonna need my help someday
Well, if you can't quit your sinnin'
Please quit your low down ways

Well, you can run down to the White House
You can gaze at the Capitol Dome, pretty mama
You can pound on the President's gate
But you oughta know by now it's gonna be too late

You're gonna need
You're gonna need my help someday
Well, if you can't quit your sinnin'
Please quit your low down ways

Well, you can run down to the desert
Throw yourself on the burning sand
You can raise up your right hand, pretty mama
But you better understand you done lost your one good
    man

You're gonna need
You're gonna need my help someday
Well, if you can't quit your sinnin'

Please quit your low down ways

And you can hitchhike on the highway
You can stand all alone by the side of the road
You can try to flag a ride back home, pretty mama
But you can't ride in my car no more

You're gonna need
You're gonna need my help someday
Well, if you can't quit your sinnin'
Please quit your low down ways

Oh, you can read out your Bible
You can fall down on your knees, pretty mama
And pray to the Lord
But it ain't gonna do no good

You're gonna need
You're gonna need my help someday
Well, if you can't quit your sinnin'
Please quit your low down ways

在那可畏的日子我真不希望我是你 [1]

是的，你的钟会停摆

在圣彼得门前 [2]

你会问他几点钟了

他会回答："太迟了"

嘿，嘿！

我真不希望我是你

在那可畏的日子

你会开始流汗

而且没法止住

你会做一个噩梦

而且永远醒不来

嘿，嘿，嘿！

我真不希望我是你

在那可畏的日子

1.《旧约·约珥书》2:31："日头要变为黑暗，月亮要变为血，这都在耶和华大而可畏的日子未到以前。"

2. 指天堂之门。《新约·马太福音》16:19，耶稣对彼得说："我要把天国的钥匙给你……"

你会哭着要药丸

你头昏又脑涨

但是药丸比你已有的

价钱会贵很多

嘿，嘿!

我真不希望我是你

在那可畏的日子

你必须裸身步行

不能坐任何车

你会让所有的人看见

你的真面目

嘿，嘿!

我真不希望我是你

在那可畏的日子

是的，美酒到处流淌

一夸脱才五美分

你会在钱包里找一找

发现你少了一美分

嘿，嘿，嘿!

我真不希望我是你

在那可畏的日子

你会大吼又尖叫

"没有人在乎吗？"

你会听见一个声音说

"在世的时候你该听话"

嘿，嘿!

我真不希望我是你

在那可畏的日子

I'd Hate to Be You on That Dreadful Day

Well, your clock is gonna stop
At Saint Peter's gate
Ya gonna ask him what time it is
He's gonna say, "It's too late"
Hey, hey!
I'd sure hate to be you
On that dreadful day

You're gonna start to sweat
And you ain't gonna stop
You're gonna have a nightmare
And never wake up
Hey, hey, hey!
I'd sure hate to be you
On that dreadful day

You're gonna cry for pills
And your head's gonna be in a knot
But the pills are gonna cost more
Than what you've got
Hey, hey!
I'd sure hate to be you
On that dreadful day

You're gonna have to walk naked
Can't ride in no car
You're gonna let ev'rybody see
Just what you are
Hey, hey!

I'd sure hate to be you
On that dreadful day

Well, the good wine's a-flowin'
For five cents a quart
You're gonna look in your moneybags
And find you're one cent short
Hey, hey, hey!
I'd sure hate to be you
On that dreadful day

You're gonna yell and scream
"Don't anybody care?"
You're gonna hear out a voice say
"Shoulda listened when you heard the word down there"
Hey, hey!
I'd sure hate to be you
On that dreadful day

纠结困惑

我纠结在困惑里
老兄，我要死了
是啊，人那么多
要让他们满意太困难

是啊，帽子拿在手中
宝贝，我沿路走下去
我在找一个女人
她的脑袋跟我的一样纠结

是啊，我的脑袋满是问题
我的体温上升得很快
是啊，我在寻找一些答案
但是我不知道能问谁

但是我一边步行一边思索
我可怜的脚不曾停下
我看见自己的影子
醉后难受，低落，烦忧！

Mixed Up Confusion

I got mixed up confusion
Man, it's a-killin' me
Well, there's too many people
And they're all too hard to please

Well, my hat's in my hand
Babe, I'm walkin' down the line
An' I'm lookin' for a woman
Whose head's mixed up like mine

Well, my head's full of questions
My temp'rature's risin' fast
Well, I'm lookin' for some answers
But I don't know who to ask

But I'm walkin' and wonderin'
And my poor feet don't ever stop
Seein' my reflection
I'm hung over, hung down, hung up!

英雄蓝调

是啊，我的这个女朋友
我发誓她是尖叫的那一方
她要我做一个英雄
好让她向朋友炫耀

是的，她哀求，她哭泣
昨夜她整晚都在求我
是的，她哀求，她哭泣
昨夜她整晚都在求我
她要我出门
找个人打架

她书读得太多
脑子里满是新电影
她书读得太多
脑子里满是电影
她要我出门用跑的
她要我爬回家死掉

宝贝，你需要的是另一种男人

那种能捉住和握住你的心的

宝贝，你需要的是另一种男人

那种能握住和捉住你的心的

宝贝，你需要的是另一种男人

你需要的是拿破仑·波泥巴[1]

是的，当我翘辫子后

我不再渴望好日子

当我翘辫子后

我不再渴望好日子

你可以站着大叫英雄

在我寂寞的坟上

---

1. 正确名字是拿破仑·波拿巴(Napoléon Bonaparte)，迪伦故意把名字拼错。

Hero Blues

Yes, the gal I got
I swear she's the screaming end
She wants me to be a hero
So she can tell all her friends.

Well, she begged, she cried
She pleaded with me all last night
Well, she begged, she cried
She pleaded with me all last night
She wants me to go out
And find somebody to fight

She reads too many books
She got new movies inside her head
She reads too many books
She got movies inside her head
She wants me to walk out running
She wants me to crawl back dead

You need a different kinda man, babe
One that can grab and hold your heart
Need a different kind of man, babe
One that can hold and grab your heart
You need a different kind of man, babe
You need Napoleon Boneeparte

Well, when I'm dead
No more good times will I crave
When I'm dead

No more good times will I crave
You can stand and shout hero
All over my lonesome grave

明天很长

如果今天不是无尽头的公路
如果今夜不是弯曲的小径
如果明天不是那么长
寂寞两字就对你毫无意义
是的，只有当我的真爱在等待
是的，而且我听见她温柔的心跳
只有当她睡在我身旁
我才会再次躺在我的床上

流水里我看不见自己的投影
我无法发出不带痛苦的声音
我听不见自己脚步的回音
也不记得自己名字的发音
是的，只有当我的真爱在等待
是的，而且我听见她温柔的心跳
只有当她睡在我身旁
我才会再次躺在我的床上

潺潺的银色河流里有美
旭日初升的天空里有美

但是这些和其他都不及

记忆中我的真爱眼睛里的美

是的，只有当我的真爱在等待

是的，而且我听见她温柔的心跳

只有当她睡在我身旁

我才会再次躺在我的床上

Tomorrow Is a Long Time

If today was not an endless highway
If tonight was not a crooked trail
If tomorrow wasn't such a long time
Then lonesome would mean nothing to you at all
Yes, and only if my own true love was waitin'
Yes, and if I could hear her heart a-softly poundin'
Only if she was lyin' by me
Then I'd lie in my bed once again

I can't see my reflection in the waters
I can't speak the sounds that show no pain
I can't hear the echo of my footsteps
Or can't remember the sound of my own name
Yes, and only if my own true love was waitin'
Yes, and if I could hear her heart a-softly poundin'
Only if she was lyin' by me
Then I'd lie in my bed once again

There's beauty in the silver, singin' river
There's beauty in the sunrise in the sky
But none of these and nothing else can touch the beauty
That I remember in my true love's eyes
Yes, and only if my own true love was waitin'
Yes, and if I could hear her heart a-softly poundin'
Only if she was lyin' by me
Then I'd lie in my bed once again

鲍勃·迪伦的新奥尔良小调

我坐在一截木桩上

在南方的新奥尔良

我的心情有点低落

人很肮脏又挺恶劣

迎面走来一个家伙

他连问也不问一声

说："我认识一个女人

能让你心情好转"

我连想都不用想

理所当然地回答

"那我们去找这位女士

她对我会有帮助"

我们一起过了河

坐在一条小船里

然后我们来到一扇门前

门牌是一〇三

我正要抬起手

轻轻地敲声门

里面走出一个家伙

连走路都很困难

一条腿在地上拖

站也站不太稳

他悲叹又呻吟

然后拖着脚走到大街

是啊，门里又出来

另外一个男人

他抖动他摇摆

他几乎站不稳

他的眼睛里

有一种恐惧

好像他才跟熊打过一架

马上就要死翘翘

我从钥匙孔看进去

看见厅堂里走过来

一个长腿的男人

他似乎无法爬行

他开口很含糊

说些破法语

他好像被

活动扳手伺候过

是啊，到了这个时候

我吓得不敢敲门

我吓得不敢动弹

处在惊吓的状态

我哼着一段小曲

拖着双脚移动

然后开始倒退

倒退到大街上

是啊，我走到街口

努力挤出一个微笑

在拐角处转身

跑了他妈的一英里

兄弟，我跑走

不是因为我病了

我跑走只是为了

赶快离开那儿

是啊，就这样我一路跑

胸腔呼哧地喘气

我得跑一英里

在一分钟以内

我踩到一截木头

又绊倒在木桩上

我赶上一列快车
只手抓紧跳上去
所以，如果你旅行
路过路易斯安那州
如果你觉得有点寂寞
或需要一个歇脚处
兄弟，你宁可活在
自己的悲惨中
也胜过对付那住在
一〇三号的女士

Bob Dylan's New Orleans Rag

I was sittin' on a stump
Down in New Orleans
I was feelin' kinda low down
Dirty and mean
Along came a fella
And he didn't even ask
He says, "I know of a woman
That can fix you up fast"
I didn't think twice
I said like I should
"Let's go find this lady
That can do me some good"
We walked across the river
On a sailin' spree
And we came to a door
Called one-oh-three

I was just about ready
To give it a little knock
When out comes a fella
Who couldn't even walk
He's linkin' and a-slinkin'
Couldn't stand on his feet
And he moaned and he groaned
And he shuffled down the street
Well, out of the door
There comes another man
He wiggled and he wobbled
He couldn't hardly stand

He had this frightened
Look in his eyes
Like he just fought a bear
He was ready to die

Well, I peeked through the key crack
Comin' down the hall
Was a long-legged man
Who couldn't hardly crawl
He muttered and he uttered
In broken French
And he looked like he'd been through
A monkey wrench

Well, by this time
I was a-scared to knock
I was a-scared to move
I's in a state of shock
I hummed a little tune
And I shuffled my feet
And I started walkin' backwards
Down that broad street
Well, I got to the corner
I tried my best to smile
I turned around the corner
And I ran a bloody mile
Man, I wasn't runnin'
'Cause I was sick
I was just a-runnin'
To get out of there quick

Well, I tripped right along
And I'm a-wheezin' in my chest

I musta run a mile
In a minute or less
I walked on a log
And I tripped on a stump
I caught a fast freight
With a one-arm jump
So, if you're travelin' down
Louisiana way
And you feel kinda lonesome
And you need a place to stay
Man, you're better off
In your misery
Than to tackle that lady
At one-oh-three

全是因为你

是啊，如果我不得不重新来过
宝贝，全是因为你我会那么做
如果我必须等待一万年
宝贝，连那我也心甘情愿
是啊，一只狗在胡同里找到骨头
一只猫，它有九条命
百万富翁有美金百万
沙特国王有王妃四百
是啊，每个人都有
他期盼的东西
我期盼我能重新来过
宝贝，我做这全都是因为你

是啊，如果今天或明天我如愿以偿
宝贝，我会四周绕着圈跑
我会在风中跳跃翻跟斗旋转
甚至在地上跳支快舞
每个人都有属于自己的时刻
每个人都有自己的时机

年少的大卫拾起石头时 [1]

甚至参孙盲了双眼之后 [2]

是啊，每个人都有机会

做他们想做的事

当我的时刻来临你最好拼了命跑

因为宝贝，我做这全都是因为你

是啊，我不需要财富，我只要一个晴天

宝贝，我的日子终会来到

我喝上一品脱酒，你知道我是巨人

当你听见我大叫："嘻哈嗬哄" [3]

是啊，你把我剪碎像一幅拼图

你让我变成一个活死人

然后你把我的心挤出脊椎骨

然后你从脖子上砍掉我的头

是啊，一旦我能够站稳

做我想做的事

1.《旧约·撒母耳记上》17:40-51，少年大卫从溪中选了五块光滑石子，以
机弦甩石击败了非利士巨人歌利亚。

2.《旧约·士师记》16:21-30，参孙因头发而有奇力，但他的情人大利拉趁
他睡觉时剃除发绺，他失去力气，被非利士人拿下，剜去双目。参孙求告耶和
华赐力，在非利士人宴上推倒房柱，同归于尽。

3. 嘻哈嗬哄，引自英国童话《杰克与魔豆茎》(Jack and the Beanstalk)，
源出一首古老的四行诗。

告诉你小情人你最好快去找掩护

因为宝贝，我做这全都是因为你

我在你门外休息因为我不想迟到

妈妈，我只是独自待着

从窗子看出去你就会看见我蹲在那儿

我净是在含含糊糊咕哝自语

是啊，等我抽完香烟

等我的酒都喝光了

等我的梦都做完了

等所有想法都想完了

是啊，等我做完了这些事

我就要去做我必须做的事

顺便告诉你，你最好跑去躲起来

因为宝贝，我做这全都是因为你

All Over You

Well, if I had to do it all over again
Babe, I'd do it all over you
And if I had to wait for ten thousand years
Babe, I'd even do that too
Well, a dog's got his bone in the alley
A cat, she's got nine lives
A millionaire's got a million dollars
King Saud's got four hundred wives
Well, ev'rybody's got somethin'
That they're lookin' forward to
I'm lookin' forward to when I can do it all again
And babe, I'll do it all over you

Well, if I had my way tomorrow or today
Babe, I'd run circles all around
I'd jump up in the wind, do a somersault and spin
I'd even dance a jig on the ground
Well, everybody gets their hour
Everybody gets their time
Little David when he picked up his pebbles
Even Sampson after he went blind
Well, everybody gets the chance
To do what they want to do
When my time arrives you better run for your life
'Cause babe, I'll do it all over you

Well, I don't need no money, I just need a day that's sunny
Baby, and my days are gonna come
And I grab me a pint, you know that I'm a giant

When you hear me yellin', "Fee-fi-fo-fum"
Well, you cut me like a jigsaw puzzle
You made me to a walkin' wreck
Then you pushed my heart through my backbone
Then you knocked off my head from my neck
Well, if I'm ever standin' steady
A-doin' what I want to do
Well, I tell you little lover that you better run for cover
'Cause babe, I'll do it all over you

I'm just restin' at your gate so that I won't be late
And, momma, I'm a-just sittin' on the shelf
Look out your window fair and you'll see me squattin' there
Just a-fumblin' and a-mumblin' to myself
Well, after my cigarette's been smoked up
After all my liquor's been drunk
After my dreams are dreamed out
After all my thoughts have been thunk
Well, after I do some of these things
I'm gonna do what I have to do
And I tell you on the side, that you better run and hide
'Cause babe, I'll do it all over you

约翰·布朗

约翰·布朗从军到外国去打仗
他的母亲真以他为傲！
穿着军服他看上去高大又挺拔
母亲看了眉开又眼笑

"哦儿子，你好帅，真高兴你是我的儿子
知道你手握长枪，我觉得好骄傲
要听队长的话，你就会得到好多勋章
等你回家后我们把它们挂在墙上"

当老火车缓缓驶出站，约翰的母亲开始叫
她要告诉所有的邻居：
"那出发的是我的儿子，他是军人，你们知道"
她务使所有的邻居都晓得

每隔一阵子她会接到来信她笑开颜
她把信拿给隔壁的邻居看
一面夸耀她的儿子穿着制服配着枪
还有那些你称之为老式战争的东西

哦！老式的战争！

然后信不再来，隔了好久都没一封信
至少有十个月都没有信
然后终于来了一封信："去车站迎接火车
你的儿子从战场回来了"

带着微笑她立刻起身，到了那儿她四处张望
但是看不到她从军的儿子
等所有的人都走了，她终于看见她的儿子
但是她不敢相信她的眼睛

哦他脸上布满了伤疤一只手也给炸没了
他的腰部还围着一道金属支架
他低声慢慢说话，她听不出他的声音
连他的脸她都认不出来！

哦！主啊！连脸都认不出来

"哦告诉我，我亲爱的儿子，求你告诉我他们做了什么
你怎么会落到这般光景？"
他挣扎着想说话，但是他的嘴巴动不了
母亲难过得把脸转过去

"妈，你还记得当初我去从军的时候
你认为那是我能做的最好的事？
我在战场上，你在家里……以我为傲
你不会了解我的处境"

"哦，在战场上我想，上帝，我在这儿做什么？
我努力杀人或为了杀人而死
最让我害怕的是，当敌人和我靠近时
我看见他的脸和我的没两样"

哦！主啊！和我的没两样！

"而且我无法不想，在炮火雷鸣腥臭的战场上
我不过是戏里的一个傀儡
在轰隆隆声和战火硝烟中，这根线终于断了
一枚加农炮弹炸瞎了我的双眼"

当他转身走开，他的母亲仍然处在惊吓中
看着那帮助他站立的金属支架
但是当他转身要走，他呼唤母亲到身边
他把他的勋章放在她手中

John Brown

John Brown went off to war to fight on a foreign shore
His mama sure was proud of him!
He stood straight and tall in his uniform and all
His mama's face broke out all in a grin

"Oh son, you look so fine, I'm glad you're a son of mine
You make me proud to know you hold a gun
Do what the captain says, lots of medals you will get
And we'll put them on the wall when you come home"

As that old train pulled out, John's ma began to shout
Tellin' ev'ryone in the neighborhood:
"That's my son that's about to go, he's a soldier now, you
   know"
She made well sure her neighbors understood

She got a letter once in a while and her face broke into a smile
As she showed them to the people from next door
And she bragged about her son with his uniform and gun
And these things you called a good old-fashioned war

Oh! Good old-fashioned war!

Then the letters ceased to come, for a long time they did not
   come
They ceased to come for about ten months or more
Then a letter finally came saying, "Go down and meet the
   train
Your son's a-coming home from the war"

She smiled and went right down, she looked everywhere
   around
But she could not see her soldier son in sight
But as all the people passed, she saw her son at last
When she did she could hardly believe her eyes

Oh his face was all shot up and his hand was all blown off
And he wore a metal brace around his waist
He whispered kind of slow, in a voice she did not know
While she couldn't even recognize his face!

Oh! Lord! Not even recognize his face

"Oh tell me, my darling son, pray tell me what they done
How is it you come to be this way?"
He tried his best to talk but his mouth could hardly move
And the mother had to turn her face away

"Don't you remember, Ma, when I went off to war
You thought it was the best thing I could do?
I was on the battleground, you were home… acting proud
You wasn't there standing in my shoes"

"Oh, and I thought when I was there, God, what am I
   doing here?
I'm a-tryin' to kill somebody or die tryin'
But the thing that scared me most was when my enemy
   came close
And I saw that his face looked just like mine"

Oh! Lord! Just like mine!

"And I couldn't help but think, through the thunder rolling
    and stink
That I was just a puppet in a play
And through the roar and smoke, this string is finally broke
And a cannonball blew my eyes away"

As he turned away to walk, his Ma was still in shock
At seein' the metal brace that helped him stand
But as he turned to go, he called his mother close
And he dropped his medals down into her hand

告别

哦请珍重，我忠贞的爱人
凌晨的第一时刻我就要离去
我将起身前往墨西哥湾
或者去加利福尼亚海岸
所以请珍重，我忠贞的爱人
某月某日我们还会再相见
并不是离别
令我忧伤
而是我真心所爱的你得留下

哦，天气跟我作对风刮得好大
滴滴雨水凝成了冰雹
往西的公路上我可能幸运搭上便车
尽管我走的是一条许多人走过的路
所以请珍重，我忠贞的爱人
某月某日我们还会再相见
并不是离别
令我忧伤
而是我真心所爱的你得留下

每隔一阵子我会给你写信
仿佛你也可以跟我一起旅行
我的脑袋，我的心和手，我的爱
我会把我学到的寄回家给你
所以请珍重，我忠贞的爱人
某月某日我们还会再相见
并不是离别
令我忧伤
而是我真心所爱的你得留下

我会告诉你那些欢笑和烦恼
不管是别人的还是我的
我双手埋在口袋里衣领立着
我将是个没人注意没人识的旅者
所以请珍重，我忠贞的爱人
某月某日我们还会再相见
并不是离别
令我忧伤
而是我真心所爱的你得留下

动身去那传说中的小镇
大概在老墨西哥平原一带
他们说那里的人很友善

他们只会问你姓甚名谁

所以请珍重，我忠贞的爱人

某月某日我们还会再见

并不是离别

令我忧伤

而是我真心所爱的你得留下

Farewell

Oh it's fare thee well my darlin' true
I'm leavin' in the first hour of the morn
I'm bound off for the bay of Mexico
Or maybe the coast of Californ
So it's fare thee well my own true love
We'll meet another day, another time
It ain't the leavin'
That's a-grievin' me
But my true love who's bound to stay behind

Oh the weather is against me and the wind blows hard
And the rain she's a-turnin' into hail
I still might strike it lucky on a highway goin' west
Though I'm travelin' on a path beaten trail
So it's fare thee well my own true love
We'll meet another day, another time
It ain't the leavin'
That's a-grievin' me
But my true love who's bound to stay behind

I will write you a letter from time to time
As I'm ramblin' you can travel with me too
With my head, my heart and my hands, my love
I will send what I learn back home to you
So it's fare thee well my own true love
We'll meet another day, another time
It ain't the leavin'
That's a-grievin' me
But my true love who's bound to stay behind

I will tell you of the laughter and of troubles
Be them somebody else's or my own
With my hands in my pockets and my coat collar high
I will travel unnoticed and unknown
So it's fare thee well my own true love
We'll meet another day, another time
It ain't the leavin'
That's a-grievin' me
But my true love who's bound to stay behind

I've heard tell of a town where I might as well be bound
It's down around the old Mexican plains
They say that the people are all friendly there
And all they ask of you is your name
So it's fare thee well my own true love
We'll meet another day, another time
It ain't the leavin'
That's a-grievin' me
But my true love who's bound to stay behind

① I found a harmonica job I started to play
Blowing my lungs out for dollar a day
Blowed my lungs out and this side down
Boss said he liked my sound
Dollars a day's worth

②
~~I finally found me a cool job~~
~~by the~~
~~What I got me a job in a bigger place~~
~~I stuck around for a day or an hour~~
~~And I played words than a clown~~
~~better~~ After weeks of me hanging around
I got a job in this man's town
In a ~~bigger~~ better place ~~with they~~ ~~bout~~ pay
My name was even posted on the ~~door~~ outside of the glass

④ Now a very great man once said
That some people rob you with a fountain pen
It ~~took~~ didn't take you long to find out
Just what he was talking about ~~not~~ about
That — table — fork — knives — cut something

⑤
So one morning when the sun was warm
I ~~took~~ ~~off~~ this here town
I pulled my cap down over my eyes
Headed out for western skies
Goodbye N.Y Howdy East range

自由不羁的鲍勃·迪伦
The Freewheelin' Bob Dylan

陈黎　张芬龄　译

　　这张专辑发行于 1963 年 5 月 27 日。在摄于同年 2 月的封面照片上，年轻的迪伦和女友苏西·罗托洛（Suze Rotolo）依偎着走在寒冷的纽约街头，脸上洋溢着笑容。

　　专辑中有多首经典之作，如作于古巴导弹危机前夕的《暴雨将至》，以及这张专辑的第一首歌曲、日后最广为人知的《在风中飘荡》。1963 年 8 月，在马丁·路德·金发表著名演说《我有一个梦想》的游行集会上，这首歌由彼得、保罗和玛丽组合（Peter, Paul and Mary）演唱，被誉为 20 世纪 60 年代美国民权运动的圣歌。

　　此外，专辑中亦有一些歌曲是迪伦有感于和女友波折的恋情而作，如《北国女孩》《沿着公路走去》《别再多想，没事了》等。1962 年 8 月到 1963 年 1 月，苏西前往意大利佩鲁贾求学，饱受相思之苦的迪伦在给她的信中提到，"我把你写进了我的歌里"。

《自由不羁的鲍勃·迪伦》体现出迪伦早期创作旺盛的生命力，他在美国文化的沃土中恣意生长，充分吸收电影、文学等各类文化养料，亦从欧美民间传统音乐中汲取创作灵感。其独特的艺术嗅觉和社会旨趣，令该专辑歌曲题材多样化，充满了激情与想象力。他凭着巧妙的修辞、灵动的节奏与强大的气势，勾勒出20世纪60年代美国的社会图景，也刻画出鲜明的个人形象。迪伦因而被称为"一代人的代言人"，但他本人对此不以为然。

迪伦包办了这张专辑中十一首歌的词曲创作，才华备受肯定。初步的成功使他摆脱了首张专辑销量不佳的窘境，然而走红带来的困扰始终折磨着他，如同专辑封面那般坦率自在的心境亦再难复回了。

编者

在风中飘荡

一个人要走过多少路
你才会称他是人？
是啊，一只白鸽要飞过多少海洋
它才能安眠于沙滩？
是啊，加农炮弹要飞多少回
才会永远被禁止？
答案啊，朋友，在风中飘荡
答案在风中飘荡

一座山能存在多少年
在被冲刷入海之前？
是啊，一些人能存活多少年
在获准自由之前？
是啊，一个人能掉头多少回
假装什么都没看见？
答案啊，朋友，在风中飘荡
答案在风中飘荡

一个人要抬头多少回
才看得到天际？

是啊，一个人要有几只耳朵

才听得到人们哭泣？

是啊，要多少人丧命，他才知道

已有太多人死去？

答案啊，朋友，在风中飘荡

答案在风中飘荡

Blowin' in the Wind

How many roads must a man walk down
Before you call him a man?
Yes, 'n' how many seas must a white dove sail
Before she sleeps in the sand?
Yes, 'n' how many times must the cannonballs fly
Before they're forever banned?
The answer, my friend, is blowin' in the wind
The answer is blowin' in the wind

How many years can a mountain exist
Before it's washed to the sea?
Yes, 'n' how many years can some people exist
Before they're allowed to be free?
Yes, 'n' how many times can a man turn his head
Pretending he just doesn't see?
The answer, my friend, is blowin' in the wind
The answer is blowin' in the wind

How many times must a man look up
Before he can see the sky?
Yes, 'n' how many ears must one man have
Before he can hear people cry?
Yes, 'n' how many deaths will it take till he knows
That too many people have died?
The answer, my friend, is blowin' in the wind
The answer is blowin' in the wind

北国女孩

啊，假如你正在阵阵强风
吹打边界的北国集市旅游
请代我问候住在那里的一个人儿
她是我真心爱过的女孩

啊，如果你去的时候雪花纷飞
河川结冰，夏日已尽
请看看她是否穿着够暖的外套
足以抵御呼号的寒风

请帮我看看她是否留着长发
是否卷曲如浪在她的胸前飘动
请帮我看看她是否留着长发
那是我记忆里她最美的模样

我想知道她是否还记得我
好多好多次我常祈祷
在黑暗的夜晚
在明亮的白昼

所以，假如你正在阵阵强风

吹打边界的北国集市旅游

请代我问候住在那里的一个人儿

她是我真心爱过的女孩

Girl of the North Country

Well, if you're travelin' in the north country fair
Where the winds hit heavy on the borderline
Remember me to one who lives there
She once was a true love of mine

Well, if you go when the snowflakes storm
When the rivers freeze and summer ends
Please see if she's wearing a coat so warm
To keep her from the howlin' winds

Please see for me if her hair hangs long
If it rolls and flows all down her breast
Please see for me if her hair hangs long
That's the way I remember her best

I'm a-wonderin' if she remembers me at all
Many times I've often prayed
In the darkness of my night
In the brightness of my day

So if you're travelin' in the north country fair
Where the winds hit heavy on the borderline
Remember me to one who lives there
She once was a true love of mine

战争大师 [1]

来吧，你们这些战争大师

你们造了所有的枪支

你们造了死亡飞机

你们造了大型炮弹

你们躲在高墙背后

你们躲在桌子背后

我只想让你们知道

我可以看穿你们的面具

你们一事无成

除了建造毁灭性的事物

你们玩弄我的世界

仿佛那是你们的小小玩具

你们把枪放在我手里

然后躲到我视线之外

转身离去越跑越远

---

1. 这首歌作于 1962 年底至 1963 年初，其时刚经历了古巴导弹危机。迪伦曾说："《战争大师》并非反战歌曲。它反对的是艾森豪威尔在卸任总统时提出的军工复合体。"

在快速子弹飞来之时

一如古代的犹大
你们撒谎又欺骗
你们要我相信
可以打赢世界大战
但我看穿了你们的眼
还看穿了你们的脑
一如我清楚看见流经
我家排水管的污水

你们扣紧扳机
叫别人开枪
然后你们后退旁观
当死亡人数节节高涨
你们躲在自家豪宅
当年轻人的血液
自身体流出
埋入泥泞里

你们抛出了
前所未有的恐惧
令人们害怕让孩子

来到这个世界

让未诞生、未取名的

我的婴儿受到威胁

你们不配拥有

血管中流动的血

我懂什么

竟如此出言不逊？

你们或许会说我年纪轻

你们或许会说我没学问

但有件事情我很清楚

虽然我比你们年轻

即便耶稣也不会

宽恕你们的行径

让我问你一个问题

你的钱那么管用

可以帮你买到宽恕吗？

你真觉得有钱就能？

我想你终将明白

当你的丧钟响起

你赚的所有钱财

永无法把你的灵魂买回来

我希望你死去

而且死期不远

在苍茫的午后

我会跟在你棺木后面

并且亲眼看你

下葬于黄泉之地

我会站在你的坟上

直到确定你已死无疑

Masters of War

Come you masters of war
You that build all the guns
You that build the death planes
You that build the big bombs
You that hide behind walls
You that hide behind desks
I just want you to know
I can see through your masks

You that never done nothin'
But build to destroy
You play with my world
Like it's your little toy
You put a gun in my hand
And you hide from my eyes
And you turn and run farther
When the fast bullets fly

Like Judas of old
You lie and deceive
A world war can be won
You want me to believe
But I see through your eyes
And I see through your brain
Like I see through the water
That runs down my drain

You fasten the triggers
For the others to fire

Then you set back and watch
When the death count gets higher
You hide in your mansion
As young people's blood
Flows out of their bodies
And is buried in the mud

You've thrown the worst fear
That can ever be hurled
Fear to bring children
Into the world
For threatening my baby
Unborn and unnamed
You ain't worth the blood
That runs in your veins

How much do I know
To talk out of turn
You might say that I'm young
You might say I'm unlearned
But there's one thing I know
Though I'm younger than you
Even Jesus would never
Forgive what you do

Let me ask you one question
Is your money that good
Will it buy you forgiveness
Do you think that it could
I think you will find
When your death takes its toll
All the money you made
Will never buy back your soul

And I hope that you die
And your death'll come soon
I will follow your casket
In the pale afternoon
And I'll watch while you're lowered
Down to your deathbed
And I'll stand o'er your grave
'Til I'm sure that you're dead

沿着公路走去

嗯，我正沿着公路走去
手提着行李箱
是的，我正沿着公路走去
手提着行李箱
主啊，我好想念我的宝贝
她在遥远的他乡

嗯，你的街道越来越空
主啊，你的公路越来越堵
你的街道越来越空
而你的公路越来越堵
嗯，我如是爱着那个女人
我敢说那会让我一命呜呼

嗯，我是个老赌徒
主啊，没剩多少可输
是的，我是个老赌徒
主啊，没剩多少可输
此刻我遇到了麻烦
别让我没了鞋子赤脚上路

嗯，我一定会走好运，宝贝

不然也定会拼命一搏

是的，我一定会走好运，宝贝

主啊主，我定会拼命一搏

嗯，与我在大海中间会合

让我们把这老旧公路抛诸脑后

嗯，大海带走了我的宝贝

我的宝贝偷走了我的心

是的，大海带走了我的宝贝

我的宝贝带走了我的心

她将它全部装进行李箱

主啊，她带着它去了意大利，意大利

所以，我正沿着你的公路走去

到我可怜视线能及的地方

是的，我正沿着你的公路走去

到我视线能及的地方

一路从金门大桥

走到自由女神像

Down the Highway

Well, I'm walkin' down the highway
With my suitcase in my hand
Yes, I'm walkin' down the highway
With my suitcase in my hand
Lord, I really miss my baby
She's in some far-off land

Well, your streets are gettin' empty
Lord, your highway's gettin' filled
And your streets are gettin' empty
And your highway's gettin' filled
Well, the way I love that woman
I swear it's bound to get me killed

Well, I been gamblin' so long
Lord, I ain't got much more to lose
Yes, I been gamblin' so long
Lord, I ain't got much more to lose
Right now I'm havin' trouble
Please don't take away my highway shoes

Well, I'm bound to get lucky, baby
Or I'm bound to die tryin'
Yes, I'm a-bound to get lucky, baby
Lord, Lord I'm a-bound to die tryin'
Well, meet me in the middle of the ocean
And we'll leave this ol' highway behind

Well, the ocean took my baby

My baby stole my heart from me
Yes, the ocean took my baby
My baby took my heart from me
She packed it all up in a suitcase
Lord, she took it away to Italy, Italy

So, I'm a-walkin' down your highway
Just as far as my poor eyes can see
Yes, I'm a-walkin' down your highway
Just as far as my eyes can see
From the Golden Gate Bridge
All the way to the Statue of Liberty

鲍勃·迪伦蓝调

嗯，独行侠和唐托 [1]

两人一路骑马而来

替大家摆平麻烦

替大家，除了我之外

必须有人告诉他们

我过得还不坏

噢，你们这些廉价庸俗的女人

你们的脑袋空空

我爱着一个很棒的女孩

主啊我爱她，直到我生命之终

别靠近我的门，我的窗

快快走开！

主啊，我不打算去赛车场

不去看跑车驰骋亮相

---

1. 美国作家弗兰·斯特赖克（Fran Striker）创作的一对在西部行侠仗义的虚
构人物，独行侠是一位蒙面侠客，唐托是他的印第安伙伴，最早出现在 1933
年的广播剧中，后来衍生为小说、电视剧等。

我没有任何跑车
也一点都不想拥有一辆
我可以随时漫步绕行街区

嗯，风不停地吹着我
在街上到处逍遥
手里拿着帽子
靴子穿在两脚
当心，不要踩到我

嗯，我跟你说，小子
你想和我一样
拔出你的六发左轮枪
看到银行就去抢
告诉法官这没关系，是我说的
是的！

Bob Dylan's Blues

Well, the Lone Ranger and Tonto
They are ridin' down the line
Fixin' ev'rybody's troubles
Ev'rybody's 'cept mine
Somebody musta tol' 'em
That I was doin' fine

Oh you five and ten cent women
With nothin' in your heads
I got a real gal I'm lovin'
And Lord I'll love her till I'm dead
Go away from my door and my window too
Right now

Lord, I ain't goin' down to no race track
See no sports car run
I don't have no sports car
And I don't even care to have one
I can walk anytime around the block

Well, the wind keeps a-blowin' me
Up and down the street
With my hat in my hand
And my boots on my feet
Watch out so you don't step on me

Well, lookit here buddy
You want to be like me
Pull out your six-shooter

And rob every bank you can see
Tell the judge I said it was all right
Yes!

暴雨将至 [1]

噢，我蓝眼睛的儿子，你上哪儿去了？

噢，我钟爱的少年郎，你上哪儿去了？

我曾跋涉过十二座雾蒙蒙的高山

我曾连走带爬行经六条蜿蜒的公路

我曾踏进七座阴郁森林的中央

我曾站在十二座死亡之海的面前

我曾深入离墓穴入口一万英里深的地底

一场暴雨，暴雨，暴雨，暴雨

一场暴雨将至

噢，我蓝眼睛的儿子，你看到了什么？

噢，我钟爱的少年郎，你看到了什么？

我看到一个新生儿被狼群包围

我看到一条钻石公路空无一人

我看到一根黑树枝不断滴落血水

我看到一个房间满是手持淌血榔头的男人

---

1. 这首歌作于古巴导弹危机发生前夕。迪伦表示："里面每一行其实都是一首全新歌曲的开头。但当我写时，我觉得来不及在有生之年写下所有那些歌曲，所以我尽可能都放进这首里头了。"

我看到一道白色梯子被水淹没

我看到一万名空谈者舌头断裂

我看到枪支和利剑在孩童的手里

一场暴雨，暴雨，暴雨，暴雨

一场暴雨将至

我蓝眼睛的儿子，你听见了什么？

我钟爱的少年郎，你听见了什么？

我听见隆隆雷鸣吼出一个警告

听见足以溺毙整个世界的海浪在怒号

听见一百个双手发火的鼓手

听见一万声低语却无人聆听

听见一个人饿死，听见许多人大笑

听见一个死于贫民窟的诗人的歌声

听见一个小丑在小巷里的哭声

一场暴雨，暴雨，暴雨，暴雨

一场暴雨将至

噢，我蓝眼睛的儿子，你遇见了谁？

我钟爱的少年郎，你遇见了谁？

我遇见一个孩童陪在一匹死去小马的身边

我遇见一个白人遛着一条黑狗

我遇见一个年轻妇人，身体被火焚烧

我遇见一个年轻女孩，她给我一道彩虹

我遇见一个男子，因爱而受伤

我遇见另一个男子，因恨而受伤

一场暴雨，暴雨，暴雨，暴雨

一场暴雨将至

噢，我蓝眼睛的儿子，你现在打算做什么？

噢，我钟爱的少年郎，你现在打算做什么？

我打算在开始下雨之前走人

我将走进最深的黑森林的深处

那儿有很多人，他们两手空空

那儿他们的河水里满是毒丸

那儿山谷中的家园与潮湿肮脏的监狱为邻

那儿刽子手的脸总是深藏不露

那儿饥饿是丑陋的，那儿灵魂遭人遗忘

那儿黑是唯一的颜色，那儿无是唯一的数字

我将诉说它，思索它，谈论它，呼吸它

自山岭映照出它的影像，让所有的灵魂都能看见

然后我将站在海上，直到我开始下沉

但在我开口歌唱之前，我很清楚自己要唱的歌曲

一场暴雨，暴雨，暴雨，暴雨

一场暴雨将至

A Hard Rain's A-Gonna Fall

Oh, where have you been, my blue-eyed son?
Oh, where have you been, my darling young one?
I've stumbled on the side of twelve misty mountains
I've walked and I've crawled on six crooked highways
I've stepped in the middle of seven sad forests
I've been out in front of a dozen dead oceans
I've been ten thousand miles in the mouth of a graveyard
And it's a hard, and it's a hard, it's a hard, and it's a hard
And it's a hard rain's a-gonna fall

Oh, what did you see, my blue-eyed son?
Oh, what did you see, my darling young one?
I saw a newborn baby with wild wolves all around it
I saw a highway of diamonds with nobody on it
I saw a black branch with blood that kept drippin'
I saw a room full of men with their hammers a-bleedin'
I saw a white ladder all covered with water
I saw ten thousand talkers whose tongues were all broken
I saw guns and sharp swords in the hands of young children
And it's a hard, and it's a hard, it's a hard, it's a hard
And it's a hard rain's a-gonna fall

And what did you hear, my blue-eyed son?
And what did you hear, my darling young one?
I heard the sound of a thunder, it roared out a warnin'
Heard the roar of a wave that could drown the whole world
Heard one hundred drummers whose hands were a-blazin'
Heard ten thousand whisperin' and nobody listenin'
Heard one person starve, I heard many people laughin'

Heard the song of a poet who died in the gutter
Heard the sound of a clown who cried in the alley
And it's a hard, and it's a hard, it's a hard, it's a hard
And it's a hard rain's a-gonna fall

Oh, who did you meet, my blue-eyed son?
Who did you meet, my darling young one?
I met a young child beside a dead pony
I met a white man who walked a black dog
I met a young woman whose body was burning
I met a young girl, she gave me a rainbow
I met one man who was wounded in love
I met another man who was wounded with hatred
And it's a hard, it's a hard, it's a hard, it's a hard
It's a hard rain's a-gonna fall

Oh, what'll you do now, my blue-eyed son?
Oh, what'll you do now, my darling young one?
I'm a-goin' back out 'fore the rain starts a-fallin'
I'll walk to the depths of the deepest black forest
Where the people are many and their hands are all empty
Where the pellets of poison are flooding their waters
Where the home in the valley meets the damp dirty prison
Where the executioner's face is always well hidden
Where hunger is ugly, where souls are forgotten
Where black is the color, where none is the number
And I'll tell it and think it and speak it and breathe it
And reflect it from the mountain so all souls can see it
Then I'll stand on the ocean until I start sinkin'
But I'll know my song well before I start singin'
And it's a hard, it's a hard, it's a hard, it's a hard
It's a hard rain's a-gonna fall

别再多想，没事了

宝贝，坐着呆想缘由无济于事
反正那已无关紧要
宝贝，坐着呆想缘由无济于事
如果至今你仍莫名其妙
破晓时分，你家公鸡啼叫之际
看看窗外，我将已离去
你是我继续上路的原因
别再多想，没事了

宝贝，把你的灯打开也无济于事
我从未见过那灯光
宝贝，把你的灯打开也无济于事
我在道路黑暗的那一方
虽然我仍希望你做点或说点什么东西
试着让我改变心意留下来陪你
不过我们从未有过太多的深谈
所以，别再多想，没事了

女孩，大喊我的名字无济于事
你从来不曾这么做过

女孩，大喊我的名字无济于事
你的声音不再进入我的耳朵
我一路上不停地思索追问
我曾爱过一个女人，是个孩子，他们说
我把心给了她，她要的却是我的灵魂
但别再多想，没事了

宝贝，我在那漫长孤寂的路上前行
要往何处，我真难逆测
但"再见"是过于美好的词，女孩
所以我将只说"别了"
我并非说你对我薄情义
你本可做得更好，但我不在意
你只是有点浪费我的宝贵光阴
但别再多想，没事了

Don't Think Twice, It's All Right

It ain't no use to sit and wonder why, babe
It don't matter, anyhow
An' it ain't no use to sit and wonder why, babe
If you don't know by now
When your rooster crows at the break of dawn
Look out your window and I'll be gone
You're the reason I'm trav'lin' on
Don't think twice, it's all right

It ain't no use in turnin' on your light, babe
That light I never knowed
An' it ain't no use in turnin' on your light, babe
I'm on the dark side of the road
Still I wish there was somethin' you would do or say
To try and make me change my mind and stay
We never did too much talkin' anyway
So don't think twice, it's all right

It ain't no use in callin' out my name, gal
Like you never did before
It ain't no use in callin' out my name, gal
I can't hear you anymore
I'm a-thinkin' and a-wond'rin' all the way down the road
I once loved a woman, a child I'm told
I give her my heart but she wanted my soul
But don't think twice, it's all right

I'm walkin' down that long, lonesome road, babe
Where I'm bound, I can't tell

But goodbye's too good a word, gal
So I'll just say fare thee well
I ain't sayin' you treated me unkind
You could have done better but I don't mind
You just kinda wasted my precious time
But don't think twice, it's all right

鲍勃·迪伦之梦

坐在西行的列车
我睡一觉休息片刻
我做了一个令我伤心的梦
关于自己和最初交往的友朋

我眼眶半湿地盯视着那个房间
许多午后和友朋同在那里消遣
我们在那里一起挨过多次风暴
又笑又唱直到拂晓

在我们挂帽子的老旧木造炉旁
我们说话，并且引吭高唱
我们别无所求，心满意惬
笑谈外面的世界

我们不安的心虽然冷暖尽历
却从未想过我们会老去
以为能永远坐享欢乐
但那样的运气微渺难得

分辨黑白很容易

分辨是非也同样容易

我们少有选择，也从未虑及

我们惯行的道路会破碎分歧

许多年岁月已消逝无踪

许多场赌局有输有赢

许多友朋踏上许多道路

我未能再见其中任一人物

我多想，多想，多想也是妄想

我们但能再次同坐于那房间

要价一万美元，我将毫不迟疑

欣然奉上，倘吾生能如是兮！

Bob Dylan's Dream

While riding on a train goin' west
I fell asleep for to take my rest
I dreamed a dream that made me sad
Concerning myself and the first few friends I had

With half-damp eyes I stared to the room
Where my friends and I spent many an afternoon
Where we together weathered many a storm
Laughin' and singin' till the early hours of the morn

By the old wooden stove where our hats was hung
Our words were told, our songs were sung
Where we longed for nothin' and were quite satisfied
Talkin' and a-jokin' about the world outside

With haunted hearts through the heat and cold
We never thought we could ever get old
We thought we could sit forever in fun
But our chances really was a million to one

As easy it was to tell black from white
It was all that easy to tell wrong from right
And our choices were few and the thought never hit
That the one road we traveled would ever shatter and split

How many a year has passed and gone
And many a gamble has been lost and won
And many a road taken by many a friend
And each one I've never seen again

I wish, I wish, I wish in vain
That we could sit simply in that room again
Ten thousand dollars at the drop of a hat
I'd give it all gladly if our lives could be like that

牛津镇 [1]

牛津镇啊，牛津镇

人人低头称臣

地面上不见阳光辉映

我不会去牛津镇

他来到牛津镇

枪支棍棒追攻其身

他那张棕褐色脸是众祸之本

最好离开牛津镇

牛津镇精神错乱

他来到门口，无法进到里头

他的肤色是众祸之源

对此你有何看法，我的朋友？

我和我女友，我女友的儿子

---

1. 这首歌应《小字报》（*Broadside*）发起的公开征集而作，命题为 1962 年发生的一则热点新闻：退伍老兵詹姆斯·梅雷迪思（James Meredith）在位于密西西比州牛津镇的密西西比大学注册，成为该校首名黑人学生。注册前夜，校园爆发白人骚乱，冲突中两人死亡。

我们饱尝了催泪瓦斯

我甚至不知我们为何来此

快回我们原来的地方才是

牛津镇午后时分

一首哀歌在众人口中轻哼

两个男子在密西西比月下断魂

最好有人赶快调查求证

牛津镇啊，牛津镇

人人低头称臣

地面上不见阳光辉映

我不会去牛津镇

Oxford Town

Oxford Town, Oxford Town
Ev'rybody's got their heads bowed down
The sun don't shine above the ground
Ain't a-goin' down to Oxford Town

He went down to Oxford Town
Guns and clubs followed him down
All because his face was brown
Better get away from Oxford Town

Oxford Town around the bend
He come in to the door, he couldn't get in
All because of the color of his skin
What do you think about that, my frien'?

Me and my gal, my gal's son
We got met with a tear gas bomb
I don't even know why we come
Goin' back where we come from

Oxford Town in the afternoon
Ev'rybody singin' a sorrowful tune
Two men died 'neath the Mississippi moon
Somebody better investigate soon

Oxford Town, Oxford Town
Ev'rybody's got their heads bowed down
The sun don't shine above the ground
Ain't a-goin' down to Oxford Town

可丽娜，可丽娜

可丽娜，可丽娜
女孩，这么久你上哪去啦？
可丽娜，可丽娜
女孩，这么久你上哪去啦？
我一直担心着你，宝贝
宝贝，回家吧

我有一只会吹口哨的鸟
我有一只会唱歌的鸟
我有一只会吹口哨的鸟
我有一只会唱歌的鸟
但是没有了可丽娜
生活就没意思啦

可丽娜，可丽娜
女孩，你让我牵挂
可丽娜，可丽娜
女孩，你让我牵挂
宝贝，我正想着你
我的眼泪不禁落下

Corrina, Corrina

Corrina, Corrina
Gal, where you been so long?
Corrina, Corrina
Gal, where you been so long?
I been worr'in' 'bout you, baby
Baby, please come home

I got a bird that whistles
I got a bird that sings
I got a bird that whistles
I got a bird that sings
But I ain' a-got Corrina
Life don't mean a thing

Corrina, Corrina
Gal, you're on my mind
Corrina, Corrina
Gal, you're on my mind
I'm a-thinkin' 'bout you, baby
I just can't keep from crying

亲爱的，只求你再给我一次机会

亲爱的，只求你再给我一次机会

与你相处

亲爱的，只求你再给我一次机会

和你一起做任何事

噢，我走在路上

手抱着头

我在寻找一个

需要男人担心的女人

只要你好心地帮我一个忙

只求你再给我一次机会

亲爱的，只求你再给我一次机会

搭乘你的飞机

亲爱的，只求你再给我一次机会

搭乘你的旅客列车

嗯，我四处寻找

和你一样的女孩

却遍寻不着

所以你只须

好心地帮我一个忙

只求你再给我一次机会

亲爱的，只求你再给我一次机会
与你相处
亲爱的，只求你再给我一次机会
和你一起做任何事
噢，要找个
没有男人的女人
就像寻找失落于
沙里的一根针
只要你好心地帮我一个忙
只求你再给我一次机会

Honey, Just Allow Me One More Chance

Honey, just allow me one more chance
To get along with you
Honey, just allow me one more chance
Ah'll do anything with you
Well, I'm a-walkin' down the road
With my head in my hand
I'm lookin' for a woman
Needs a worried man
Just-a one kind favor I ask you
'Low me just-a one more chance

Honey, just allow me one more chance
To ride your aeroplane
Honey, just allow me one more chance
To ride your passenger train
Well, I've been lookin' all over
For a gal like you
I can't find nobody
So you'll have to do
Just-a one kind favor I ask you
'Low me just-a one more chance

Honey, just allow me one more chance
To along with you
Honey, just allow me one more chance
Ah'll do anything with you
Well, lookin' for a woman
That ain't got no man
Is just lookin' for a needle

That is lost in the sand
Just-a one kind favor I ask you
'Low me just-a one more chance

我将无拘无束

嗯，昨天深夜我带了个女人回家
我七八分醉意，她看起来紧张焦虑
她脱掉她的轮子，脱掉她的铃铛
脱掉她的假发，说："我闻起来味道如何？"
我急急忙忙……全身赤裸……
跳窗而出！

嗯，我有时或许会喝醉
走起路来像鸭子，跺起步来像臭鼬
谁都别伤害我，别伤害我的自尊
因为我的小女士就在我身边
（就在那里
骄傲无比）

我在外头漆着老旧木棚
一罐黑漆掉落头上
我下来又擦又抹
但不得不坐到浴缸末端
（要价二十五美分
我得快点出去……

有人想进来洗个桑拿）[1]

嗯，我的电话响个不停

是肯尼迪总统打来的

他说：“鲍勃吾友，我们需要什么才能让国家茁壮？”

我说：“约翰吾友，碧姬·芭铎

安妮塔·艾克伯格

索菲亚·罗兰[2]”

（把她们和欧内斯特·博格宁[3]放在同一个房间里！）

嗯，我跟一个女人睡在吊床上

她经常又喊又吼又尖叫

舔我的脸又搔我的耳

要我俯身又买啤酒给我喝

（她是度蜜月者

六月低吟歌者

---

1. 1876 年至 1965 年间，美国南部及边境各州执行吉姆·克劳法（Jim Crow laws），实施种族隔离，例如规定黑人必须坐在交通工具的后头，并因应白人的需求让座。此节是对此的讽刺。

2. 碧姬·芭铎（Brigitte Bardot，1934— ）、安妮塔·艾克伯格（Anita Ekberg，1931—2015）和索菲亚·罗兰（Sophia Loren，1934— ）都是以性感著称的女影星。

3. 欧内斯特·博格宁（Ernest Borgnine，1917—2012），美国著名演员，凭在《君子好逑》（Marty，1955）中的演出获奥斯卡金像奖。

以汤匙喂食者

天生的领导者）

噢，我没必要劳累地工作

我有个在堤坝工作的女人

抽水工作忙得不可开交

她每周寄给我一张月兑的支票

（她是很棒的人

唱民歌的人

和那个叫什么的

酷似的人）

一星期当中某日稍晚时分

我闭着眼睛半睡半醒

我追一个女人追到山上

当时正在举行防空演习

那是牧羊女小波比！

（我跳进防核尘地下室

我跳上魔豆茎

我跳入摩天轮）

现在，台上的男人想要我的选票

他正以无记名投票竞选公职

他在尖塔前面大声疾呼

跟我说他爱各式各样的人

（他吃着百吉饼

他吃着披萨

他吃着猪肠

他吃着牛粪[1]！）

噢，安排我到电视节目现场

我会把频道转到第四台

一个成年人自淋浴间走出

手里拿着一瓶发油

（那是那油头小子的玩意儿

橄榄球先生，我想知道的是

你对威利·梅斯[2]、尤·伯连纳[3]

夏尔·戴高乐，和罗伯特·刘易斯·斯蒂文森

所知多少？）

啊，我所见过最好笑的女人

---

1. 牛粪，亦有"废话"之意。
2. 威利·梅斯（Willy Mays，1931— ），美国棒球运动员，司职中外野手，先后效力于纽约巨人队及纽约大都会队，1979年入选美国国家棒球名人堂。
3. 尤·伯连纳（Yul Brynner，1920—1985），美国俄裔演员，凭《国王与我》（*The King and I*，1956）获奥斯卡金像奖。

是科林先生[1]的曾孙女

她一天大概洗十五次澡

想要我在脸上种雪茄

（她稍稍重了点！）

嗯，你问我为什么老是喝醉酒

那让我头脑稳定心情放松

我只不过沿路走着，漫步歌唱

看更美好的日子，做更棒的事

（我捕捉恐龙

和伊丽莎白·泰勒做爱……

被理查德·伯顿[2]痛扁一顿！）

---

1. 科林先生，亦有"干净先生""清廉君子"之意。
2. 美国演员伊丽莎白·泰勒（Elizabeth Taylor，1932—2011）与理查德·伯顿（Richard Burton，1925—1984）当年因拍摄《埃及艳后》（*Cleopatra*，1962）而相恋，轰动一时。

I Shall Be Free

Well, I took me a woman late last night
I's three-fourths drunk, she looked uptight
She took off her wheel, took off her bell
Took off her wig, said, "How do I smell?"
I hot-footed it… bare-naked…
Out the window!

Well, sometimes I might get drunk
Walk like a duck and stomp like a skunk
Don't hurt me none, don't hurt my pride
'Cause I got my little lady right by my side
(Right there
Proud as can be)

I's out there paintin' on the old woodshed
When a can a black paint it fell on my head
I went down to scrub and rub
But I had to sit in back of the tub
(Cost a quarter
And I had to get out quick…
Someone wanted to come in and take a sauna)

Well, my telephone rang it would not stop
It's President Kennedy callin' me up
He said, "My friend, Bob, what do we need to make the
    country grow?"
I said, "My friend, John, Brigitte Bardot
Anita Ekberg
Sophia Loren"

(Put 'em all in the same room with Ernest Borgnine!)

Well, I got a woman sleeps on a cot
She yells and hollers and squeals a lot
Licks my face and tickles my ear
Bends me over and buys me beer
(She's a honeymooner
A June crooner
A spoon feeder
And a natural leader)

Oh, there ain't no use in me workin' so heavy
I got a woman who works on the levee
Pumping that water up to her neck
Every week she sends me a monthly check
(She's a humdinger
Folk singer
Dead ringer
For a thing-a-muh jigger)

Late one day in the middle of the week
Eyes were closed I was half asleep
I chased me a woman up the hill
Right in the middle of an air-raid drill
It was Little Bo Peep!
(I jumped a fallout shelter
I jumped a bean stalk
I jumped a Ferris wheel)

Now, the man on the stand he wants my vote
He's a-runnin' for office on the ballot note
He's out there preachin' in front of the steeple
Tellin' me he loves all kinds-a people

(He's eatin' bagels
He's eatin' pizza
He's eatin' chitlins
He's eatin' bullshit!)

Oh, set me down on a television floor
I'll flip the channel to number four
Out of the shower comes a grown-up man
With a bottle of hair oil in his hand
(It's that greasy kid stuff
What I want to know, Mr. Football Man, is
What do you do about Willy Mays and YulBrynner
Charles de Gaulle
And Robert Louis Stevenson?)

Well, the funniest woman I ever seen
Was the great-granddaughter of Mr. Clean
She takes about fifteen baths a day
Wants me to grow a cigar on my face
(She's a little bit heavy!)

Well, ask me why I'm drunk alla time
It levels my head and eases my mind
I just walk along and stroll and sing
I see better days and I do better things
(I catch dinosaurs
I make love to Elizabeth Taylor...
Catch hell from Richard Burton!)

你打算怎么做

告诉我你打算怎么做
当阴影出现于你家门缝？
告诉我你打算怎么做
当阴影出现于你家门缝？
告诉我你打算怎么做
当阴影出现于你家门缝？
主啊，主啊
你会怎么做？

告诉我你打算怎么做
当魔鬼向你叫牌？
告诉我你打算怎么做
当魔鬼向你叫牌？
告诉我你打算怎么做
当魔鬼向你叫牌？
主啊，主啊
你会怎么做？

告诉我你打算怎么做

当你的水变成了酒？[1]

告诉我你打算怎么做

当你的水变成了酒？

告诉我你打算怎么做

当你的水变成了酒？

主啊，主啊

你该怎么做？

告诉我你打算怎么做

当你再也不能扮演神的角色？

告诉我你打算怎么做

当你再也不能扮演神的角色？

告诉我你打算怎么做

当你再也不能扮演神的角色？

主啊，主啊

你会怎么做？

告诉我你打算怎么做

当阴影爬进你的房里？

告诉我你打算怎么做

当阴影爬进你的房里？

1.《新约·约翰福音》2:7-9，耶稣在筵席上变水为酒。

告诉我你打算怎么做

当阴影爬进你的房里？

主啊，主啊

你该怎么做？

Whatcha Gonna Do

Tell me what you're gonna do
When the shadow comes under your door
Tell me what you're gonna do
When the shadow comes under your door
Tell me what you're gonna do
When the shadow comes under your door
O Lord, O Lord
What shall you do?

Tell me what you're gonna do
When the devil calls your cards
Tell me what you're gonna do
When the devil calls your cards
Tell me what you're gonna do
When the devil calls your cards
O Lord, O Lord
What shall you do?

Tell me what you're gonna do
When your water turns to wine
Tell me what you're gonna do
When your water turns to wine
Tell me what you're gonna do
When your water turns to wine
O Lord, O Lord
What should you do?

Tell me what you're gonna do
When you can't play God no more

Tell me what you're gonna do
When you can't play God no more
Tell me what you're gonna do
When you can't play God no more
O Lord, O Lord
What shall you do?

Tell me what you're gonna do
When the shadow comes creepin' in your room
Tell me what you're gonna do
When the shadow comes creepin' in your room
Tell me what you're gonna do
When the shadow comes creepin' in your room
O Lord, O Lord
What should you do?

红翼之墙 [1]

噢，同居舍友的年龄

我粗略地记得：

不小于十二

不大于十七

像盗匪一样被丢入

像罪犯一样被抛出

在高墙之内

红翼之墙

你从又脏又旧的食堂

大步走到砖墙

倦得不想交谈

累得唱不了歌

噢，一整个下午

你想念着家乡

在高墙之内

红翼之墙

---

1. 指美国明尼苏达州的红翼镇（又译作"雷德温"）少管所，歌词内容全属迪
伦的想象，并非实情。

噢，大门铸上了铁

高墙架设了带刺铁丝

远离那篱笆

它通了刺人的电流

低下你的头

待在号码里

在高墙之内

红翼之墙

噢，告别

深凹的地窖

告别带你走向

屏幕的木栈道

告别他们以此威胁你的

时时刻刻

在高墙之内

红翼之墙

有许多警卫

站在四周微笑

手握棍棒

仿佛自己是国王

希望在木桩背后

将你逮个正着

在高墙之内

红翼之墙

夜将阴影投入

横条围起的窗户

风用力地敲击

让墙板唱起歌来

好多个夜晚

我假装熟睡

在高墙之内

红翼之墙

雨哗啦哗啦地打在

工寮的木瓦屋顶上

夜晚的声音

在我耳边作响

直到警卫的钥匙

咔嗒响起清晨的旋律

在高墙之内

红翼之墙

噢，我们当中有些最后

被关进圣克劳德市监狱

我们当中有些后来

做了律师之类的工作

我们当中有些会挺身而出

与你们在十字路口相见

自高墙之内

红翼之墙

Walls of Red Wing

Oh, the age of the inmates
I remember quite freely:
No younger than twelve
No older 'n seventeen
Thrown in like bandits
And cast off like criminals
Inside the walls
The walls of Red Wing

From the dirty old mess hall
You march to the brick wall
Too weary to talk
And too tired to sing
Oh, it's all afternoon
You remember your hometown
Inside the walls
The walls of Red Wing

Oh, the gates are cast iron
And the walls are barbed wire
Stay far from the fence
With the 'lectricity sting
And it's keep down your head
And stay in your number
Inside the walls
The walls of Red Wing

Oh, it's fare thee well
To the deep hollow dungeon

Farewell to the boardwalk
That takes you to the screen
And farewell to the minutes
They threaten you with it
Inside the walls
The walls of Red Wing

It's many a guard
That stands around smilin'
Holdin' his club
Like he was a king
Hopin' to get you
Behind a wood pilin'
Inside the walls
The walls of Red Wing

The night aimed shadows
Through the crossbar windows
And the wind punched hard
To make the wall-siding sing
It's many a night
I pretended to be a-sleepin'
Inside the walls
The walls of Red Wing

As the rain rattled heavy
On the bunkhouse shingles
And the sounds in the night
They made my ears ring
'Til the keys of the guards
Clicked the tune of the morning
Inside the walls
The walls of Red Wing

Oh, some of us'll end up
In St. Cloud Prison
And some of us'll wind up
To be lawyers and things
And some of us'll stand up
To meet you on your crossroads
From inside the walls
The walls of Red Wing

谁杀了戴维·摩尔[1]？

谁杀了戴维·摩尔？
为什么，原因为何？

"不是我，"裁判说
"别用手指指着我
我本可以在第八回合叫停
或许让他逃过命运
但观众会发出嘘声，我敢保证
说并未值回票价
他非死不可太不幸了
但我也有压力在身，你知道的
不是我使他倒下的
不，你绝不可以怪我"

谁杀了戴维·摩尔？
为什么，原因为何？

---

1. 戴维·摩尔（Davey Moore，1933—1963），美国次轻量级拳击手，曾获世界冠军，1963 年在比赛中头部受伤致死。

"不是我们，"尖叫声响彻
拳击场的愤怒观众说
"他那晚死去太不幸了
但我们只不过爱看打斗
并无意要他赴死
我们只不过想看到一些汗水
这没什么不对！
不是我们使他倒下的
不，你绝不可以怪我们"

谁杀了戴维·摩尔？
为什么，原因为何？

"不是我，"抽着大雪茄
吞云吐雾的他的经纪人说
"这很难说，这难以预料
我一直以为他身体很好
他死了，他的妻儿太不幸了
但他如果有病，应该早点说
不是我使他倒下的
不，你绝不可以怪我"

谁杀了戴维·摩尔？

为什么，原因为何？

"不是我，"手里还捏着
票根的赌徒说
"不是我将他击倒的
我的手根本没碰到他
我并未犯下丑陋罪行
反正，我赌的是他会赢
不是我使他倒下的
不，你绝不可以怪我"

谁杀了戴维·摩尔？
为什么，原因为何？

"不是我，"拳击作家说
一边在旧打字机上敲打印刷字体
一边说："拳击没有错
橄榄球比赛也一样危险"
又说："搏击在此落地生根
这不过是行之有年的美国式拳术
不是我使他倒下的
不，你绝不可以怪我"

谁杀了戴维·摩尔？
为什么，原因为何？

"不是我，"用拳头将他摆平
于一团迷雾之中的男人说
他走出古巴国门来到这里
拳击在该国已不再被允许
"我打了他，是的，没错
但我是受雇工作
别说成'谋杀'，别说成'杀害'
那是命运，上帝的旨意"

谁杀了戴维·摩尔？
为什么，原因为何？

Who Killed Davey Moore?

Who killed Davey Moore
Why an' what's the reason for?

"Not I," says the referee
"Don't point your finger at me
I could've stopped it in the eighth
An' maybe kept him from his fate
But the crowd would've booed, I'm sure
At not gettin' their money's worth
It's too bad he had to go
But there was a pressure on me too, you know
It wasn't me that made him fall
No, you can't blame me at all"

Who killed Davey Moore
Why an' what's the reason for?

"Not us," says the angry crowd
Whose screams filled the arena loud
"It's too bad he died that night
But we just like to see a fight
We didn't mean for him t' meet his death
We just meant to see some sweat
There ain't nothing wrong in that
It wasn't us that made him fall
No, you can't blame us at all"

Who killed Davey Moore
Why an' what's the reason for?

"Not me," says his manager
Puffing on a big cigar
"It's hard to say, it's hard to tell
I always thought that he was well
It's too bad for his wife an' kids he's dead
But if he was sick, he should've said
It wasn't me that made him fall
No, you can't blame me at all"

Who killed Davey Moore
Why an' what's the reason for?

"Not me," says the gambling man
With his ticket stub still in his hand
"It wasn't me that knocked him down
My hands never touched him none
I didn't commit no ugly sin
Anyway, I put money on him to win
It wasn't me that made him fall
No, you can't blame me at all"

Who killed Davey Moore
Why an' what's the reason for?

"Not me," says the boxing writer
Pounding print on his old typewriter
Sayin', "Boxing ain't to blame
There's just as much danger in a football game"
Sayin', "Fistfighting is here to stay
It's just the old American way
It wasn't me that made him fall
No, you can't blame me at all"

Who killed Davey Moore
Why an' what's the reason for?

"Not me," says the man whose fists
Laid him low in a cloud of mist
Who came here from Cuba's door
Where boxing ain't allowed no more
"I hit him, yes, it's true
But that's what I am paid to do
Don't say 'murder,' don't say 'kill'
It was destiny, it was God's will"

Who killed Davey Moore
Why an' what's the reason for?

七个诅咒

老赖利偷了匹种马
他们抓到他，把他带回来
叫他躺到牢房的地上
用铁链缠住他的脖子

老赖利的女儿得知消息
她父亲将被处以绞刑
她连夜骑马，清晨抵达
手里拿着金子和银子

当法官见到赖利的女儿
他那双老眼深陷于头颅
他说："金子释放不了你父亲
亲爱的，你才是救命的代价"

"噢，我死定了，"赖利哭着说
"他想要的只是你
他只要碰你一下，我全身起疙瘩
你快快骑上马离开"

"噢，父亲，你一定会死
如果我不冒险一试
付出代价，不听你劝告
为此我必须留下"

绞刑台的影子撼动黄昏
入夜后猎犬咆哮
入夜后大地呻吟
入夜后付出了代价

第二天早晨她醒来后
始知法官一句话也没说
她看到绞刑支架弯曲
她看到父亲的尸体残破

送此恶毒法官七个诅咒：
一个医生救不了他
两名医者治不好他
三只眼睛看不到他

四只耳朵也听不见他
五面墙壁也藏不住他
六名掘墓人也葬不了他
七次死亡还便宜了他！

Seven Curses

Old Reilly stole a stallion
But they caught him and they brought him back
And they laid him down on the jailhouse ground
With an iron chain around his neck

Old Reilly's daughter got a message
That her father was goin' to hang
She rode by night and came by morning
With gold and silver in her hand

When the judge he saw Reilly's daughter
His old eyes deepened in his head
Sayin', "Gold will never free your father
The price, my dear, is you instead"

"Oh I'm as good as dead," cried Reilly
"It's only you that he does crave
And my skin will surely crawl if he touches you at all
Get on your horse and ride away"

"Oh father you will surely die
If I don't take the chance to try
And pay the price and not take your advice
For that reason I will have to stay"

The gallows shadows shook the evening
In the night a hound dog bayed
In the night the grounds were groanin'
In the night the price was paid

The next mornin' she had awoken
To know that the judge had never spoken
She saw that hangin' branch a-bendin'
She saw her father's body broken

These be seven curses on a judge so cruel:
That one doctor will not save him
That two healers will not heal him
That three eyes will not see him

That four ears will not hear him
That five walls will not hide him
That six diggers will not bury him
And that seven deaths shall never kill him

尘土飞扬的老露天游乐场

嗯，初春时分我们自佛罗里达一路北上
卡车和拖车将蜿蜒而行
我们像子弹一般朝嘉年华路线发射
我们听从尘土飞扬的老露天游乐场的召唤

从密歇根淤泥经过威斯康星太阳
跨越明尼苏达边界，一路向前奔波
穿过清澈的县湖和伐木区
我们听从尘土飞扬的老露天游乐场的召唤

颠簸到法戈，再南下到阿伯丁
翻越老布莱克山，一路向前推进
穿过牛乡小镇和老蒙大拿的砂土
我们听从露天游乐场的召唤

当公路上的白线在你车轮底下悠游
我凝望拖车车窗大笑
啊，我们衣裳虽破但色泽鲜艳
听从尘土飞扬的老露天游乐场的召唤

弯弯曲曲的路上结识许多朋友

杂耍卖艺人、骗子、赌徒

嗯，我和算命师之类的人共度时光

听从露天游乐场的召唤

噢，打下横木，绑好帐篷

让帆布旗帜飞扬

嗯，让"毛毛虫"[1]旋转，上紧摩天轮的发条

听从露天游乐场的召唤

嗯，驶进镇里直奔露天游乐场

就在挂有宣传海报的后头

随处挤满不一样的脸孔

听从露天游乐场的召唤

把跳舞的女孩排到前头，把赌博表演摆后头

听旧音乐盒发出隆隆乐声

听小孩，面容，微笑在中间走道来来去去

我们听从露天游乐场的召唤

在镇上一直待到活动的最后一刻

---

1. "毛毛虫"，一种游乐场中的旋转车。

早上再开上熟悉的公路

不去多想，准时把自己载往下一个小镇

听从露天游乐场的召唤

口琴在寂寞的夜晚泣诉

我们一边前行一边喝着红酒

我转了许多个弯，学到了许多教训

因为听从露天游乐场的召唤

驾车回到圣彼得兹堡

系好拖车，就地露营

把我们所赚的钱用来支付场租费

听从尘土飞扬的老露天游乐场的召唤

Dusty Old Fairgrounds

Well, it's all up from Florida at the start of the spring
The trucks and the trailers will be winding
Like a bullet we'll shoot for the carnival route
We're following them dusty old fairgrounds a-calling

From the Michigan mud past the Wisconsin sun
'Cross that Minnesota border, keep 'em scrambling
Through the clear county lakes and the lumberjack lands
We're following them dusty old fairgrounds a-calling

Hit Fargo on the jump and down to Aberdeen
'Cross them old Black Hills, keep 'em rolling
Through the cow country towns and the sands of old
 Montana
We're following them fairgrounds a-calling

As the white line on the highway sails under your wheels
I've gazed from the trailer window laughing
Oh, our clothes they was torn but the colors they was bright
Following them dusty old fairgrounds a-calling

It's a-many a friend that follows the bend
The jugglers, the hustlers, the gamblers
Well, I've spent my time with the fortune-telling kind
Following them fairgrounds a-calling

Oh, it's pound down the rails and it's tie down the tents
Get that canvas flag a-flying
Well, let the caterpillars spin, let the Ferris wheel wind

Following them fairgrounds a-calling

Well, it's roll into town straight to the fairgrounds
Just behind the posters that are hanging
And it's fill up every space with a different kind of face
Following them fairgrounds a-calling

Get the dancing girls in front, get the gambling show
    behind
Hear that old music box a-banging
Hear them kids, faces, smiles, up and down the midway
    aisles
We're following them fairgrounds a-calling

It's a-drag it on down by the deadline in the town
Hit the old highway by the morning
And it's ride yourself blind for the next town on time
Following them fairgrounds a-calling

As the harmonicas whined in the lonesome nighttime
Drinking red wine as we're rolling
Many a turnin' I turn, many a lesson I learn
From following them fairgrounds a-calling

And it's roll back down to St. Petersburg
Tie down the trailers and camp 'em
And the money that we made will pay for the space
From following them dusty old fairgrounds a-calling